– Tax Checklist –

Name _____

Financial Year _____

- ☐ Tax ID / social security number/ tax file number: _____
- ☐ Previous year's tax statements

INCOME

- ☐ Day Job ☐ _____
- ☐ Bank account details ☐ _____
- ☐ Bank statements ☐ _____
- ☐ Dividends on investments ☐ _____
- ☐ Business income ☐ _____
- ☐ Blog income ☐ _____
- ☐ Foreign income ☐ _____
- ☐ Investment property income ☐ _____

EXPENSES

- ☐ Day Job ☐ _____
- ☐ Business ☐ _____
- ☐ Blog ☐ _____
- ☐ Investment property ☐ _____
- ☐ Charity ☐ _____
- ☐ Medical ☐ _____
- ☐ Interest paid on loans ☐ _____
- ☐ Child /Children relared expenses ☐ _____

Note: _____

_____

- Tax Checklist -

Name _____

Financial Year _____

- ☐ Tax ID / social security number/ tax file number: _____
- ☐ Previous year's tax statements

INCOME

- ☐ Day Job ☐ _____
- ☐ Bank account details ☐ _____
- ☐ Bank statements ☐ _____
- ☐ Dividends on investments ☐ _____
- ☐ Business income ☐ _____
- ☐ Blog income ☐ _____
- ☐ Foreign income ☐ _____
- ☐ Investment property income ☐ _____

EXPENSES

- ☐ Day Job ☐ _____
- ☐ Business ☐ _____
- ☐ Blog ☐ _____
- ☐ Investment property ☐ _____
- ☐ Charity ☐ _____
- ☐ Medical ☐ _____
- ☐ Interest paid on loans ☐ _____
- ☐ Child /Children relared expenses ☐ _____

Note: _____

_____

_____

- Tax Checklist -

Name _____

Financial Year _____

- ☐ Tax ID / social security number/ tax file number: _____
- ☐ Previous year's tax statements

INCOME

- ☐ Day Job   ☐ _____
- ☐ Bank account details ☐ _____
- ☐ Bank statements   ☐ _____
- ☐ Dividends on investments ☐ _____
- ☐ Business income   ☐ _____
- ☐ Blog income   ☐ _____
- ☐ Foreign income   ☐ _____
- ☐ Investment property income ☐ _____

EXPENSES

- ☐ Day Job   ☐ _____
- ☐ Business   ☐ _____
- ☐ Blog   ☐ _____
- ☐ Investment property ☐ _____
- ☐ Charity   ☐ _____
- ☐ Medical   ☐ _____
- ☐ Interest paid on loans ☐ _____
- ☐ Child /Children relared expenses ☐ _____

Note: _____
_____
_____

– Tax Checklist –

Name _____

Financial Year _____

- ☐ Tax ID / social security number/ tax file number: _____
- ☐ Previous year's tax statements

INCOME

- ☐ Day Job ☐ _____
- ☐ Bank account details ☐ _____
- ☐ Bank statements ☐ _____
- ☐ Dividends on investments ☐ _____
- ☐ Business income ☐ _____
- ☐ Blog income ☐ _____
- ☐ Foreign income ☐ _____
- ☐ Investment property income ☐ _____

EXPENSES

- ☐ Day Job ☐ _____
- ☐ Business ☐ _____
- ☐ Blog ☐ _____
- ☐ Investment property ☐ _____
- ☐ Charity ☐ _____
- ☐ Medical ☐ _____
- ☐ Interest paid on loans ☐ _____
- ☐ Child /Children relared expenses ☐ _____

Note: _____

- Tax Checklist -

Name _____

Financial Year _____

- ☐ Tax ID / social security number/ tax file number: _____
- ☐ Previous year's tax statements

INCOME

- ☐ Day Job ☐ _____
- ☐ Bank account details ☐ _____
- ☐ Bank statements ☐ _____
- ☐ Dividends on investments ☐ _____
- ☐ Business income ☐ _____
- ☐ Blog income ☐ _____
- ☐ Foreign income ☐ _____
- ☐ Investment property income ☐ _____

EXPENSES

- ☐ Day Job ☐ _____
- ☐ Business ☐ _____
- ☐ Blog ☐ _____
- ☐ Investment property ☐ _____
- ☐ Charity ☐ _____
- ☐ Medical ☐ _____
- ☐ Interest paid on loans ☐ _____
- ☐ Child /Children relared expenses ☐ _____

Note: _____

− Tax Checklist −

Name _____

Financial Year _____

- ☐ Tax ID / social security number/ tax file number: _____
- ☐ Previous year's tax statements

INCOME

- ☐ Day Job   ☐ _____
- ☐ Bank account details   ☐ _____
- ☐ Bank statements   ☐ _____
- ☐ Dividends on investments   ☐ _____
- ☐ Business income   ☐ _____
- ☐ Blog income   ☐ _____
- ☐ Foreign income   ☐ _____
- ☐ Investment property income   ☐ _____

EXPENSES

- ☐ Day Job   ☐ _____
- ☐ Business   ☐ _____
- ☐ Blog   ☐ _____
- ☐ Investment property   ☐ _____
- ☐ Charity   ☐ _____
- ☐ Medical   ☐ _____
- ☐ Interest paid on loans   ☐ _____
- ☐ Child /Children relared expenses ☐ _____

Note: _____

– Tax Checklist –

Name _____

Financial Year _____

- ☐ Tax ID / social security number/ tax file number: _____
- ☐ Previous year's tax statements

INCOME

- ☐ Day Job ☐ _____
- ☐ Bank account details ☐ _____
- ☐ Bank statements ☐ _____
- ☐ Dividends on investments ☐ _____
- ☐ Business income ☐ _____
- ☐ Blog income ☐ _____
- ☐ Foreign income ☐ _____
- ☐ Investment property income ☐ _____

EXPENSES

- ☐ Day Job ☐ _____
- ☐ Business ☐ _____
- ☐ Blog ☐ _____
- ☐ Investment property ☐ _____
- ☐ Charity ☐ _____
- ☐ Medical ☐ _____
- ☐ Interest paid on loans ☐ _____
- ☐ Child /Children relared expenses ☐ _____

Note: _____

- Tax Checklist -

Name _____

Financial Year _____

- ☐ Tax ID / social security number/ tax file number: _____
- ☐ Previous year's tax statements

INCOME

- ☐ Day Job   ☐ _____
- ☐ Bank account details   ☐ _____
- ☐ Bank statements   ☐ _____
- ☐ Dividends on investments   ☐ _____
- ☐ Business income   ☐ _____
- ☐ Blog income   ☐ _____
- ☐ Foreign income   ☐ _____
- ☐ Investment property income   ☐ _____

EXPENSES

- ☐ Day Job   ☐ _____
- ☐ Business   ☐ _____
- ☐ Blog   ☐ _____
- ☐ Investment property   ☐ _____
- ☐ Charity   ☐ _____
- ☐ Medical   ☐ _____
- ☐ Interest paid on loans   ☐ _____
- ☐ Child /Children relared expenses ☐ _____

Note: _____

– Tax Checklist –

Name _____

Financial Year _____

- ☐ Tax ID / social security number/ tax file number: _____
- ☐ Previous year's tax statements

INCOME

- ☐ Day Job   ☐ _____
- ☐ Bank account details   ☐ _____
- ☐ Bank statements   ☐ _____
- ☐ Dividends on investments   ☐ _____
- ☐ Business income   ☐ _____
- ☐ Blog income   ☐ _____
- ☐ Foreign income   ☐ _____
- ☐ Investment property income   ☐ _____

EXPENSES

- ☐ Day Job   ☐ _____
- ☐ Business   ☐ _____
- ☐ Blog   ☐ _____
- ☐ Investment property   ☐ _____
- ☐ Charity   ☐ _____
- ☐ Medical   ☐ _____
- ☐ Interest paid on loans   ☐ _____
- ☐ Child /Children relared expenses   ☐ _____

Note: _____

— Tax Checklist —

Name _____

Financial Year _____

- ☐ Tax ID / social security number/ tax file number: _____
- ☐ Previous year's tax statements

INCOME

- ☐ Day Job ☐ _____
- ☐ Bank account details ☐ _____
- ☐ Bank statements ☐ _____
- ☐ Dividends on investments ☐ _____
- ☐ Business income ☐ _____
- ☐ Blog income ☐ _____
- ☐ Foreign income ☐ _____
- ☐ Investment property income ☐ _____

EXPENSES

- ☐ Day Job ☐ _____
- ☐ Business ☐ _____
- ☐ Blog ☐ _____
- ☐ Investment property ☐ _____
- ☐ Charity ☐ _____
- ☐ Medical ☐ _____
- ☐ Interest paid on loans ☐ _____
- ☐ Child /Children relared expenses ☐ _____

Note: _____

- Tax Checklist -

Name _____

Financial Year _____

- ☐ Tax ID / social security number/ tax file number: _____
- ☐ Previous year's tax statements

INCOME

- ☐ Day Job   ☐ _____
- ☐ Bank account details   ☐ _____
- ☐ Bank statements   ☐ _____
- ☐ Dividends on investments   ☐ _____
- ☐ Business income   ☐ _____
- ☐ Blog income   ☐ _____
- ☐ Foreign income   ☐ _____
- ☐ Investment property income   ☐ _____

EXPENSES

- ☐ Day Job   ☐ _____
- ☐ Business   ☐ _____
- ☐ Blog   ☐ _____
- ☐ Investment property   ☐ _____
- ☐ Charity   ☐ _____
- ☐ Medical   ☐ _____
- ☐ Interest paid on loans   ☐ _____
- ☐ Child /Children relared expenses ☐ _____

Note: _____

_____

_____

– Tax Checklist –

Name _____

Financial Year _____

- ☐ Tax ID / social security number/ tax file number: _____
- ☐ Previous year's tax statements

INCOME

- ☐ Day Job   ☐ _____
- ☐ Bank account details   ☐ _____
- ☐ Bank statements   ☐ _____
- ☐ Dividends on investments   ☐ _____
- ☐ Business income   ☐ _____
- ☐ Blog income   ☐ _____
- ☐ Foreign income   ☐ _____
- ☐ Investment property income   ☐ _____

EXPENSES

- ☐ Day Job   ☐ _____
- ☐ Business   ☐ _____
- ☐ Blog   ☐ _____
- ☐ Investment property   ☐ _____
- ☐ Charity   ☐ _____
- ☐ Medical   ☐ _____
- ☐ Interest paid on loans   ☐ _____
- ☐ Child /Children relared expenses   ☐ _____

Note: _____

_____

_____

- Tax Checklist -

Name _____

Financial Year _____

- ☐ Tax ID / social security number/ tax file number: _____
- ☐ Previous year's tax statements

INCOME

- ☐ Day Job ☐ _____
- ☐ Bank account details ☐ _____
- ☐ Bank statements ☐ _____
- ☐ Dividends on investments ☐ _____
- ☐ Business income ☐ _____
- ☐ Blog income ☐ _____
- ☐ Foreign income ☐ _____
- ☐ Investment property income ☐ _____

EXPENSES

- ☐ Day Job ☐ _____
- ☐ Business ☐ _____
- ☐ Blog ☐ _____
- ☐ Investment property ☐ _____
- ☐ Charity ☐ _____
- ☐ Medical ☐ _____
- ☐ Interest paid on loans ☐ _____
- ☐ Child /Children relared expenses ☐ _____

Note: _____

_____

_____

- Tax Checklist -

Name _____

Financial Year _____

☐ Tax ID / social security number/ tax file number: _____

☐ Previous year's tax statements

INCOME

☐ Day Job ☐ _____
☐ Bank account details ☐ _____
☐ Bank statements ☐ _____
☐ Dividends on investments ☐ _____
☐ Business income ☐ _____
☐ Blog income ☐ _____
☐ Foreign income ☐ _____
☐ Investment property income ☐ _____

EXPENSES

☐ Day Job ☐ _____
☐ Business ☐ _____
☐ Blog ☐ _____
☐ Investment property ☐ _____
☐ Charity ☐ _____
☐ Medical ☐ _____
☐ Interest paid on loans ☐ _____
☐ Child /Children relared expenses ☐ _____

Note: _____
_____
_____

- Tax Checklist -

Name _____

Financial Year _____

- ☐ Tax ID / social security number/ tax file number: _____
- ☐ Previous year's tax statements

INCOME

- ☐ Day Job ☐ _____
- ☐ Bank account details ☐ _____
- ☐ Bank statements ☐ _____
- ☐ Dividends on investments ☐ _____
- ☐ Business income ☐ _____
- ☐ Blog income ☐ _____
- ☐ Foreign income ☐ _____
- ☐ Investment property income ☐ _____

EXPENSES

- ☐ Day Job ☐ _____
- ☐ Business ☐ _____
- ☐ Blog ☐ _____
- ☐ Investment property ☐ _____
- ☐ Charity ☐ _____
- ☐ Medical ☐ _____
- ☐ Interest paid on loans ☐ _____
- ☐ Child /Children relared expenses ☐ _____

Note: _____
_____

- Tax Checklist -

Name _____

Financial Year _____

- ☐ Tax ID / social security number/ tax file number: _____
- ☐ Previous year's tax statements

INCOME

- ☐ Day Job   ☐ _____
- ☐ Bank account details   ☐ _____
- ☐ Bank statements   ☐ _____
- ☐ Dividends on investments   ☐ _____
- ☐ Business income   ☐ _____
- ☐ Blog income   ☐ _____
- ☐ Foreign income   ☐ _____
- ☐ Investment property income   ☐ _____

EXPENSES

- ☐ Day Job   ☐ _____
- ☐ Business   ☐ _____
- ☐ Blog   ☐ _____
- ☐ Investment property   ☐ _____
- ☐ Charity   ☐ _____
- ☐ Medical   ☐ _____
- ☐ Interest paid on loans   ☐ _____
- ☐ Child /Children relared expenses   ☐ _____

Note: _____

_____

_____

- Tax Checklist -

Name _____

Financial Year _____

- ☐ Tax ID / social security number/ tax file number: _____
- ☐ Previous year's tax statements

INCOME

- ☐ Day Job   ☐ _____
- ☐ Bank account details   ☐ _____
- ☐ Bank statements   ☐ _____
- ☐ Dividends on investments   ☐ _____
- ☐ Business income   ☐ _____
- ☐ Blog income   ☐ _____
- ☐ Foreign income   ☐ _____
- ☐ Investment property income   ☐ _____

EXPENSES

- ☐ Day Job   ☐ _____
- ☐ Business   ☐ _____
- ☐ Blog   ☐ _____
- ☐ Investment property   ☐ _____
- ☐ Charity   ☐ _____
- ☐ Medical   ☐ _____
- ☐ Interest paid on loans   ☐ _____
- ☐ Child /Children relared expenses ☐ _____

Note: _____

_____

_____

- *Tax Checklist* -

Name _____

Financial Year _____

- ☐ Tax ID / social security number/ tax file number: _____
- ☐ Previous year's tax statements

INCOME

- ☐ Day Job ☐ _____
- ☐ Bank account details ☐ _____
- ☐ Bank statements ☐ _____
- ☐ Dividends on investments ☐ _____
- ☐ Business income ☐ _____
- ☐ Blog income ☐ _____
- ☐ Foreign income ☐ _____
- ☐ Investment property income ☐ _____

EXPENSES

- ☐ Day Job ☐ _____
- ☐ Business ☐ _____
- ☐ Blog ☐ _____
- ☐ Investment property ☐ _____
- ☐ Charity ☐ _____
- ☐ Medical ☐ _____
- ☐ Interest paid on loans ☐ _____
- ☐ Child /Children relared expenses ☐ _____

Note: _____

_____

_____

- Tax Checklist -

Name _____

Financial Year _____

- ☐ Tax ID / social security number/ tax file number: _____
- ☐ Previous year's tax statements

INCOME

- ☐ Day Job   ☐ _____
- ☐ Bank account details   ☐ _____
- ☐ Bank statements   ☐ _____
- ☐ Dividends on investments   ☐ _____
- ☐ Business income   ☐ _____
- ☐ Blog income   ☐ _____
- ☐ Foreign income   ☐ _____
- ☐ Investment property income   ☐ _____

EXPENSES

- ☐ Day Job   ☐ _____
- ☐ Business   ☐ _____
- ☐ Blog   ☐ _____
- ☐ Investment property   ☐ _____
- ☐ Charity   ☐ _____
- ☐ Medical   ☐ _____
- ☐ Interest paid on loans   ☐ _____
- ☐ Child /Children relared expenses ☐ _____

Note: _____

_____

_____

- Tax Checklist -

Name _____

Financial Year _____

- ☐ Tax ID / social security number/ tax file number: _____
- ☐ Previous year's tax statements

INCOME

- ☐ Day Job ☐ _____
- ☐ Bank account details ☐ _____
- ☐ Bank statements ☐ _____
- ☐ Dividends on investments ☐ _____
- ☐ Business income ☐ _____
- ☐ Blog income ☐ _____
- ☐ Foreign income ☐ _____
- ☐ Investment property income ☐ _____

EXPENSES

- ☐ Day Job ☐ _____
- ☐ Business ☐ _____
- ☐ Blog ☐ _____
- ☐ Investment property ☐ _____
- ☐ Charity ☐ _____
- ☐ Medical ☐ _____
- ☐ Interest paid on loans ☐ _____
- ☐ Child /Children relared expenses ☐ _____

Note: _____

_____

- Tax Checklist -

Name _____

Financial Year _____

- ☐ Tax ID / social security number/ tax file number: _____
- ☐ Previous year's tax statements

INCOME

- ☐ Day Job ☐ _____
- ☐ Bank account details ☐ _____
- ☐ Bank statements ☐ _____
- ☐ Dividends on investments ☐ _____
- ☐ Business income ☐ _____
- ☐ Blog income ☐ _____
- ☐ Foreign income ☐ _____
- ☐ Investment property income ☐ _____

EXPENSES

- ☐ Day Job ☐ _____
- ☐ Business ☐ _____
- ☐ Blog ☐ _____
- ☐ Investment property ☐ _____
- ☐ Charity ☐ _____
- ☐ Medical ☐ _____
- ☐ Interest paid on loans ☐ _____
- ☐ Child /Children relared expenses ☐ _____

Note: _____
_____
_____

– Tax Checklist –

Name _____

Financial Year _____

☐ Tax ID / social security number/ tax file number: _____

☐ Previous year's tax statements

INCOME

☐ Day Job   ☐ _____
☐ Bank account details   ☐ _____
☐ Bank statements   ☐ _____
☐ Dividends on investments   ☐ _____
☐ Business income   ☐ _____
☐ Blog income   ☐ _____
☐ Foreign income   ☐ _____
☐ Investment property income   ☐ _____

EXPENSES

☐ Day Job   ☐ _____
☐ Business   ☐ _____
☐ Blog   ☐ _____
☐ Investment property   ☐ _____
☐ Charity   ☐ _____
☐ Medical   ☐ _____
☐ Interest paid on loans   ☐ _____
☐ Child /Children relared expenses   ☐ _____

Note: _____

_____

_____

- Tax Checklist -

Name _____

Financial Year _____

- ☐ Tax ID / social security number/ tax file number: _____
- ☐ Previous year's tax statements

INCOME

- ☐ Day Job
- ☐ Bank account details
- ☐ Bank statements
- ☐ Dividends on investments
- ☐ Business income
- ☐ Blog income
- ☐ Foreign income
- ☐ Investment property income

☐ _____
☐ _____
☐ _____
☐ _____
☐ _____
☐ _____
☐ _____
☐ _____

EXPENSES

- ☐ Day Job
- ☐ Business
- ☐ Blog
- ☐ Investment property
- ☐ Charity
- ☐ Medical
- ☐ Interest paid on loans
- ☐ Child /Children relared expenses

☐ _____
☐ _____
☐ _____
☐ _____
☐ _____
☐ _____
☐ _____
☐ _____

Note: _____

_____

_____

- *Tax Checklist* -

Name _____

Financial Year _____

- ☐ Tax ID / social security number/ tax file number: _____
- ☐ Previous year's tax statements

INCOME

- ☐ Day Job   ☐ _____
- ☐ Bank account details   ☐ _____
- ☐ Bank statements   ☐ _____
- ☐ Dividends on investments   ☐ _____
- ☐ Business income   ☐ _____
- ☐ Blog income   ☐ _____
- ☐ Foreign income   ☐ _____
- ☐ Investment property income   ☐ _____

EXPENSES

- ☐ Day Job   ☐ _____
- ☐ Business   ☐ _____
- ☐ Blog   ☐ _____
- ☐ Investment property   ☐ _____
- ☐ Charity   ☐ _____
- ☐ Medical   ☐ _____
- ☐ Interest paid on loans   ☐ _____
- ☐ Child /Children relared expenses ☐ _____

Note: _____

_____

- Tax Checklist -

Name _____

Financial Year _____

- ☐ Tax ID / social security number/ tax file number: _____
- ☐ Previous year's tax statements

INCOME

- ☐ Day Job   ☐ _____
- ☐ Bank account details   ☐ _____
- ☐ Bank statements   ☐ _____
- ☐ Dividends on investments   ☐ _____
- ☐ Business income   ☐ _____
- ☐ Blog income   ☐ _____
- ☐ Foreign income   ☐ _____
- ☐ Investment property income   ☐ _____

EXPENSES

- ☐ Day Job   ☐ _____
- ☐ Business   ☐ _____
- ☐ Blog   ☐ _____
- ☐ Investment property   ☐ _____
- ☐ Charity   ☐ _____
- ☐ Medical   ☐ _____
- ☐ Interest paid on loans   ☐ _____
- ☐ Child /Children relared expenses   ☐ _____

Note: _____

_____

_____

– Tax Checklist –

Name _____

Financial Year _____

- ☐ Tax ID / social security number/ tax file number: _____
- ☐ Previous year's tax statements

INCOME

- ☐ Day Job   ☐ _____
- ☐ Bank account details   ☐ _____
- ☐ Bank statements   ☐ _____
- ☐ Dividends on investments   ☐ _____
- ☐ Business income   ☐ _____
- ☐ Blog income   ☐ _____
- ☐ Foreign income   ☐ _____
- ☐ Investment property income   ☐ _____

EXPENSES

- ☐ Day Job   ☐ _____
- ☐ Business   ☐ _____
- ☐ Blog   ☐ _____
- ☐ Investment property   ☐ _____
- ☐ Charity   ☐ _____
- ☐ Medical   ☐ _____
- ☐ Interest paid on loans   ☐ _____
- ☐ Child /Children relared expenses ☐ _____

Note: _____

_____

- Tax Checklist -

Name _____

Financial Year _____

- ☐ Tax ID / social security number/ tax file number: _____
- ☐ Previous year's tax statements

INCOME

- ☐ Day Job ☐ _____
- ☐ Bank account details ☐ _____
- ☐ Bank statements ☐ _____
- ☐ Dividends on investments ☐ _____
- ☐ Business income ☐ _____
- ☐ Blog income ☐ _____
- ☐ Foreign income ☐ _____
- ☐ Investment property income ☐ _____

EXPENSES

- ☐ Day Job ☐ _____
- ☐ Business ☐ _____
- ☐ Blog ☐ _____
- ☐ Investment property ☐ _____
- ☐ Charity ☐ _____
- ☐ Medical ☐ _____
- ☐ Interest paid on loans ☐ _____
- ☐ Child /Children relared expenses ☐ _____

Note: _____

_____

_____

- Tax Checklist -

Name _____

Financial Year _____

- ☐ Tax ID / social security number/ tax file number: _____
- ☐ Previous year's tax statements

INCOME

- ☐ Day Job ☐ _____
- ☐ Bank account details ☐ _____
- ☐ Bank statements ☐ _____
- ☐ Dividends on investments ☐ _____
- ☐ Business income ☐ _____
- ☐ Blog income ☐ _____
- ☐ Foreign income ☐ _____
- ☐ Investment property income ☐ _____

EXPENSES

- ☐ Day Job ☐ _____
- ☐ Business ☐ _____
- ☐ Blog ☐ _____
- ☐ Investment property ☐ _____
- ☐ Charity ☐ _____
- ☐ Medical ☐ _____
- ☐ Interest paid on loans ☐ _____
- ☐ Child /Children relared expenses ☐ _____

Note:_____
_____

– Tax Checklist –

Name _____

Financial Year _____

☐ Tax ID / social security number/ tax file number: _____
☐ Previous year's tax statements

INCOME

☐ Day Job ☐ _____
☐ Bank account details ☐ _____
☐ Bank statements ☐ _____
☐ Dividends on investments ☐ _____
☐ Business income ☐ _____
☐ Blog income ☐ _____
☐ Foreign income ☐ _____
☐ Investment property income ☐ _____

EXPENSES

☐ Day Job ☐ _____
☐ Business ☐ _____
☐ Blog ☐ _____
☐ Investment property ☐ _____
☐ Charity ☐ _____
☐ Medical ☐ _____
☐ Interest paid on loans ☐ _____
☐ Child /Children relared expenses ☐ _____

Note: _____
_____
_____

- *Tax Checklist* -

Name _____

Financial Year _____

- ☐ Tax ID / social security number/ tax file number: _____
- ☐ Previous year's tax statements

INCOME

- ☐ Day Job   ☐ _____
- ☐ Bank account details   ☐ _____
- ☐ Bank statements   ☐ _____
- ☐ Dividends on investments   ☐ _____
- ☐ Business income   ☐ _____
- ☐ Blog income   ☐ _____
- ☐ Foreign income   ☐ _____
- ☐ Investment property income   ☐ _____

EXPENSES

- ☐ Day Job   ☐ _____
- ☐ Business   ☐ _____
- ☐ Blog   ☐ _____
- ☐ Investment property   ☐ _____
- ☐ Charity   ☐ _____
- ☐ Medical   ☐ _____
- ☐ Interest paid on loans   ☐ _____
- ☐ Child /Children relared expenses ☐ _____

Note: _____

_____

_____

− Tax Checklist −

Name _____

Financial Year _____

☐ Tax ID / social security number/ tax file number: _____
☐ Previous year's tax statements

INCOME

☐ Day Job ☐ _____
☐ Bank account details ☐ _____
☐ Bank statements ☐ _____
☐ Dividends on investments ☐ _____
☐ Business income ☐ _____
☐ Blog income ☐ _____
☐ Foreign income ☐ _____
☐ Investment property income ☐ _____

EXPENSES

☐ Day Job ☐ _____
☐ Business ☐ _____
☐ Blog ☐ _____
☐ Investment property ☐ _____
☐ Charity ☐ _____
☐ Medical ☐ _____
☐ Interest paid on loans ☐ _____
☐ Child /Children relared expenses ☐ _____

Note: _____
_____

− Tax Checklist −

Name _____

Financial Year _____

☐ Tax ID / social security number/ tax file number: _____

☐ Previous year's tax statements

INCOME

☐ Day Job   ☐ _____
☐ Bank account details   ☐ _____
☐ Bank statements   ☐ _____
☐ Dividends on investments   ☐ _____
☐ Business income   ☐ _____
☐ Blog income   ☐ _____
☐ Foreign income   ☐ _____
☐ Investment property income   ☐ _____

EXPENSES

☐ Day Job   ☐ _____
☐ Business   ☐ _____
☐ Blog   ☐ _____
☐ Investment property   ☐ _____
☐ Charity   ☐ _____
☐ Medical   ☐ _____
☐ Interest paid on loans   ☐ _____
☐ Child /Children relared expenses   ☐ _____

Note: _____

– Tax Checklist –

Name _____

Financial Year _____

- ☐ Tax ID / social security number/ tax file number: _____
- ☐ Previous year's tax statements

INCOME

- ☐ Day Job   ☐ _____
- ☐ Bank account details   ☐ _____
- ☐ Bank statements   ☐ _____
- ☐ Dividends on investments   ☐ _____
- ☐ Business income   ☐ _____
- ☐ Blog income   ☐ _____
- ☐ Foreign income   ☐ _____
- ☐ Investment property income   ☐ _____

EXPENSES

- ☐ Day Job   ☐ _____
- ☐ Business   ☐ _____
- ☐ Blog   ☐ _____
- ☐ Investment property   ☐ _____
- ☐ Charity   ☐ _____
- ☐ Medical   ☐ _____
- ☐ Interest paid on loans   ☐ _____
- ☐ Child /Children relared expenses ☐ _____

Note: _____

_____

_____

- Tax Checklist -

Name _____

Financial Year _____

☐ Tax ID / social security number/ tax file number: _____
☐ Previous year's tax statements

INCOME

☐ Day Job ☐ _____
☐ Bank account details ☐ _____
☐ Bank statements ☐ _____
☐ Dividends on investments ☐ _____
☐ Business income ☐ _____
☐ Blog income ☐ _____
☐ Foreign income ☐ _____
☐ Investment property income ☐ _____

EXPENSES

☐ Day Job ☐ _____
☐ Business ☐ _____
☐ Blog ☐ _____
☐ Investment property ☐ _____
☐ Charity ☐ _____
☐ Medical ☐ _____
☐ Interest paid on loans ☐ _____
☐ Child /Children relared expenses ☐ _____

Note: _____

— Tax Checklist —

Name _____

Financial Year _____

- ☐ Tax ID / social security number/ tax file number: _____
- ☐ Previous year's tax statements

INCOME

- ☐ Day Job   ☐ _____
- ☐ Bank account details   ☐ _____
- ☐ Bank statements   ☐ _____
- ☐ Dividends on investments   ☐ _____
- ☐ Business income   ☐ _____
- ☐ Blog income   ☐ _____
- ☐ Foreign income   ☐ _____
- ☐ Investment property income   ☐ _____

EXPENSES

- ☐ Day Job   ☐ _____
- ☐ Business   ☐ _____
- ☐ Blog   ☐ _____
- ☐ Investment property   ☐ _____
- ☐ Charity   ☐ _____
- ☐ Medical   ☐ _____
- ☐ Interest paid on loans   ☐ _____
- ☐ Child /Children relared expenses ☐ _____

Note: _____

_____

_____

− Tax Checklist −

Name _____

Financial Year _____

- ☐ Tax ID / social security number/ tax file number: _____
- ☐ Previous year's tax statements

INCOME

- ☐ Day Job   ☐ _____
- ☐ Bank account details   ☐ _____
- ☐ Bank statements   ☐ _____
- ☐ Dividends on investments   ☐ _____
- ☐ Business income   ☐ _____
- ☐ Blog income   ☐ _____
- ☐ Foreign income   ☐ _____
- ☐ Investment property income   ☐ _____

EXPENSES

- ☐ Day Job   ☐ _____
- ☐ Business   ☐ _____
- ☐ Blog   ☐ _____
- ☐ Investment property   ☐ _____
- ☐ Charity   ☐ _____
- ☐ Medical   ☐ _____
- ☐ Interest paid on loans   ☐ _____
- ☐ Child /Children relared expenses   ☐ _____

Note: _____

_____

_____

- Tax Checklist -

Name _____

Financial Year _____

- ☐ Tax ID / social security number/ tax file number: _____
- ☐ Previous year's tax statements

INCOME

- ☐ Day Job   ☐ _____
- ☐ Bank account details   ☐ _____
- ☐ Bank statements   ☐ _____
- ☐ Dividends on investments   ☐ _____
- ☐ Business income   ☐ _____
- ☐ Blog income   ☐ _____
- ☐ Foreign income   ☐ _____
- ☐ Investment property income   ☐ _____

EXPENSES

- ☐ Day Job   ☐ _____
- ☐ Business   ☐ _____
- ☐ Blog   ☐ _____
- ☐ Investment property   ☐ _____
- ☐ Charity   ☐ _____
- ☐ Medical   ☐ _____
- ☐ Interest paid on loans   ☐ _____
- ☐ Child /Children relared expenses ☐ _____

Note:_____

_____

_____

- *Tax Checklist* -

Name _____

Financial Year _____

- ☐ Tax ID / social security number/ tax file number: _____
- ☐ Previous year's tax statements

INCOME

- ☐ Day Job ☐ _____
- ☐ Bank account details ☐ _____
- ☐ Bank statements ☐ _____
- ☐ Dividends on investments ☐ _____
- ☐ Business income ☐ _____
- ☐ Blog income ☐ _____
- ☐ Foreign income ☐ _____
- ☐ Investment property income ☐ _____

EXPENSES

- ☐ Day Job ☐ _____
- ☐ Business ☐ _____
- ☐ Blog ☐ _____
- ☐ Investment property ☐ _____
- ☐ Charity ☐ _____
- ☐ Medical ☐ _____
- ☐ Interest paid on loans ☐ _____
- ☐ Child /Children relared expenses ☐ _____

Note: _____

_____

_____

– Tax Checklist –

Name _____

Financial Year _____

- ☐ Tax ID / social security number/ tax file number: _____
- ☐ Previous year's tax statements

INCOME

- ☐ Day Job
- ☐ Bank account details
- ☐ Bank statements
- ☐ Dividends on investments
- ☐ Business income
- ☐ Blog income
- ☐ Foreign income
- ☐ Investment property income

☐ _____
☐ _____
☐ _____
☐ _____
☐ _____
☐ _____
☐ _____
☐ _____

EXPENSES

- ☐ Day Job
- ☐ Business
- ☐ Blog
- ☐ Investment property
- ☐ Charity
- ☐ Medical
- ☐ Interest paid on loans
- ☐ Child /Children relared expenses

☐ _____
☐ _____
☐ _____
☐ _____
☐ _____
☐ _____
☐ _____
☐ _____

Note: _____

- *Tax Checklist* -

Name _____

Financial Year _____

- ☐ Tax ID / social security number/ tax file number: _____
- ☐ Previous year's tax statements

INCOME

- ☐ Day Job ☐ _____
- ☐ Bank account details ☐ _____
- ☐ Bank statements ☐ _____
- ☐ Dividends on investments ☐ _____
- ☐ Business income ☐ _____
- ☐ Blog income ☐ _____
- ☐ Foreign income ☐ _____
- ☐ Investment property income ☐ _____

EXPENSES

- ☐ Day Job ☐ _____
- ☐ Business ☐ _____
- ☐ Blog ☐ _____
- ☐ Investment property ☐ _____
- ☐ Charity ☐ _____
- ☐ Medical ☐ _____
- ☐ Interest paid on loans ☐ _____
- ☐ Child /Children relared expenses ☐ _____

Note: _____

_____

_____

– Tax Checklist –

Name _____

Financial Year _____

- ☐ Tax ID / social security number/ tax file number: _____
- ☐ Previous year's tax statements

INCOME

- ☐ Day Job   ☐ _____
- ☐ Bank account details   ☐ _____
- ☐ Bank statements   ☐ _____
- ☐ Dividends on investments   ☐ _____
- ☐ Business income   ☐ _____
- ☐ Blog income   ☐ _____
- ☐ Foreign income   ☐ _____
- ☐ Investment property income   ☐ _____

EXPENSES

- ☐ Day Job   ☐ _____
- ☐ Business   ☐ _____
- ☐ Blog   ☐ _____
- ☐ Investment property   ☐ _____
- ☐ Charity   ☐ _____
- ☐ Medical   ☐ _____
- ☐ Interest paid on loans   ☐ _____
- ☐ Child /Children relared expenses   ☐ _____

Note: _____

_____
_____

– Tax Checklist –

Name _____

Financial Year _____

- ☐ Tax ID / social security number/ tax file number: _____
- ☐ Previous year's tax statements

INCOME

- ☐ Day Job   ☐ _____
- ☐ Bank account details   ☐ _____
- ☐ Bank statements   ☐ _____
- ☐ Dividends on investments   ☐ _____
- ☐ Business income   ☐ _____
- ☐ Blog income   ☐ _____
- ☐ Foreign income   ☐ _____
- ☐ Investment property income   ☐ _____

EXPENSES

- ☐ Day Job   ☐ _____
- ☐ Business   ☐ _____
- ☐ Blog   ☐ _____
- ☐ Investment property   ☐ _____
- ☐ Charity   ☐ _____
- ☐ Medical   ☐ _____
- ☐ Interest paid on loans   ☐ _____
- ☐ Child /Children relared expenses ☐ _____

Note: _____

− Tax Checklist −

Name _____

Financial Year _____

- ☐ Tax ID / social security number/ tax file number: _____
- ☐ Previous year's tax statements

INCOME

- ☐ Day Job   ☐ _____
- ☐ Bank account details   ☐ _____
- ☐ Bank statements   ☐ _____
- ☐ Dividends on investments   ☐ _____
- ☐ Business income   ☐ _____
- ☐ Blog income   ☐ _____
- ☐ Foreign income   ☐ _____
- ☐ Investment property income   ☐ _____

EXPENSES

- ☐ Day Job   ☐ _____
- ☐ Business   ☐ _____
- ☐ Blog   ☐ _____
- ☐ Investment property   ☐ _____
- ☐ Charity   ☐ _____
- ☐ Medical   ☐ _____
- ☐ Interest paid on loans   ☐ _____
- ☐ Child /Children relared expenses   ☐ _____

Note: _____

_____

_____

− Tax Checklist −

Name _____

Financial Year _____

- ☐ Tax ID / social security number/ tax file number: _____
- ☐ Previous year's tax statements

INCOME

- ☐ Day Job ☐ _____
- ☐ Bank account details ☐ _____
- ☐ Bank statements ☐ _____
- ☐ Dividends on investments ☐ _____
- ☐ Business income ☐ _____
- ☐ Blog income ☐ _____
- ☐ Foreign income ☐ _____
- ☐ Investment property income ☐ _____

EXPENSES

- ☐ Day Job ☐ _____
- ☐ Business ☐ _____
- ☐ Blog ☐ _____
- ☐ Investment property ☐ _____
- ☐ Charity ☐ _____
- ☐ Medical ☐ _____
- ☐ Interest paid on loans ☐ _____
- ☐ Child /Children relared expenses ☐ _____

Note: _____

_____

- *Tax Checklist* -

Name _____

Financial Year _____

- ☐ Tax ID / social security number/ tax file number: _____
- ☐ Previous year's tax statements

INCOME

- ☐ Day Job   ☐ _____
- ☐ Bank account details   ☐ _____
- ☐ Bank statements   ☐ _____
- ☐ Dividends on investments   ☐ _____
- ☐ Business income   ☐ _____
- ☐ Blog income   ☐ _____
- ☐ Foreign income   ☐ _____
- ☐ Investment property income   ☐ _____

EXPENSES

- ☐ Day Job   ☐ _____
- ☐ Business   ☐ _____
- ☐ Blog   ☐ _____
- ☐ Investment property   ☐ _____
- ☐ Charity   ☐ _____
- ☐ Medical   ☐ _____
- ☐ Interest paid on loans   ☐ _____
- ☐ Child /Children relared expenses   ☐ _____

Note: _____

_____

_____

- Tax Checklist -

Name _____

Financial Year _____

- ☐ Tax ID / social security number/ tax file number: _____
- ☐ Previous year's tax statements

INCOME

- ☐ Day Job ☐ _____
- ☐ Bank account details ☐ _____
- ☐ Bank statements ☐ _____
- ☐ Dividends on investments ☐ _____
- ☐ Business income ☐ _____
- ☐ Blog income ☐ _____
- ☐ Foreign income ☐ _____
- ☐ Investment property income ☐ _____

EXPENSES

- ☐ Day Job ☐ _____
- ☐ Business ☐ _____
- ☐ Blog ☐ _____
- ☐ Investment property ☐ _____
- ☐ Charity ☐ _____
- ☐ Medical ☐ _____
- ☐ Interest paid on loans ☐ _____
- ☐ Child /Children relared expenses ☐ _____

Note: _____

– Tax Checklist –

Name _____

Financial Year _____

- ☐ Tax ID / social security number/ tax file number: _____
- ☐ Previous year's tax statements

INCOME

- ☐ Day Job   ☐ _____
- ☐ Bank account details   ☐ _____
- ☐ Bank statements   ☐ _____
- ☐ Dividends on investments   ☐ _____
- ☐ Business income   ☐ _____
- ☐ Blog income   ☐ _____
- ☐ Foreign income   ☐ _____
- ☐ Investment property income   ☐ _____

EXPENSES

- ☐ Day Job   ☐ _____
- ☐ Business   ☐ _____
- ☐ Blog   ☐ _____
- ☐ Investment property   ☐ _____
- ☐ Charity   ☐ _____
- ☐ Medical   ☐ _____
- ☐ Interest paid on loans   ☐ _____
- ☐ Child /Children relared expenses ☐ _____

Note: _____

_____

- Tax Checklist -

Name _____

Financial Year _____

- ☐ Tax ID / social security number/ tax file number: _____
- ☐ Previous year's tax statements

INCOME

- ☐ Day Job ☐ _____
- ☐ Bank account details ☐ _____
- ☐ Bank statements ☐ _____
- ☐ Dividends on investments ☐ _____
- ☐ Business income ☐ _____
- ☐ Blog income ☐ _____
- ☐ Foreign income ☐ _____
- ☐ Investment property income ☐ _____

EXPENSES

- ☐ Day Job ☐ _____
- ☐ Business ☐ _____
- ☐ Blog ☐ _____
- ☐ Investment property ☐ _____
- ☐ Charity ☐ _____
- ☐ Medical ☐ _____
- ☐ Interest paid on loans ☐ _____
- ☐ Child /Children relared expenses ☐ _____

Note: _____

- Tax Checklist -

Name _____

Financial Year _____

☐ Tax ID / social security number/ tax file number: _____
☐ Previous year's tax statements

INCOME

☐ Day Job ☐ _____
☐ Bank account details ☐ _____
☐ Bank statements ☐ _____
☐ Dividends on investments ☐ _____
☐ Business income ☐ _____
☐ Blog income ☐ _____
☐ Foreign income ☐ _____
☐ Investment property income ☐ _____

EXPENSES

☐ Day Job ☐ _____
☐ Business ☐ _____
☐ Blog ☐ _____
☐ Investment property ☐ _____
☐ Charity ☐ _____
☐ Medical ☐ _____
☐ Interest paid on loans ☐ _____
☐ Child /Children relared expenses ☐ _____

Note: _____

_____

- Tax Checklist -

Name _____

Financial Year _____

- ☐ Tax ID / social security number/ tax file number: _____
- ☐ Previous year's tax statements

INCOME

- ☐ Day Job ☐ _____
- ☐ Bank account details ☐ _____
- ☐ Bank statements ☐ _____
- ☐ Dividends on investments ☐ _____
- ☐ Business income ☐ _____
- ☐ Blog income ☐ _____
- ☐ Foreign income ☐ _____
- ☐ Investment property income ☐ _____

EXPENSES

- ☐ Day Job ☐ _____
- ☐ Business ☐ _____
- ☐ Blog ☐ _____
- ☐ Investment property ☐ _____
- ☐ Charity ☐ _____
- ☐ Medical ☐ _____
- ☐ Interest paid on loans ☐ _____
- ☐ Child /Children relared expenses ☐ _____

Note: _____

_____

– Tax Checklist –

Name _____

Financial Year _____

- ☐ Tax ID / social security number/ tax file number: _____
- ☐ Previous year's tax statements

INCOME

- ☐ Day Job   ☐ _____
- ☐ Bank account details   ☐ _____
- ☐ Bank statements   ☐ _____
- ☐ Dividends on investments   ☐ _____
- ☐ Business income   ☐ _____
- ☐ Blog income   ☐ _____
- ☐ Foreign income   ☐ _____
- ☐ Investment property income   ☐ _____

EXPENSES

- ☐ Day Job   ☐ _____
- ☐ Business   ☐ _____
- ☐ Blog   ☐ _____
- ☐ Investment property   ☐ _____
- ☐ Charity   ☐ _____
- ☐ Medical   ☐ _____
- ☐ Interest paid on loans   ☐ _____
- ☐ Child /Children relared expenses ☐ _____

Note: _____

_____

_____

- Tax Checklist -

Name _____

Financial Year _____

- ☐ Tax ID / social security number/ tax file number: _____
- ☐ Previous year's tax statements

INCOME

- ☐ Day Job ☐ _____
- ☐ Bank account details ☐ _____
- ☐ Bank statements ☐ _____
- ☐ Dividends on investments ☐ _____
- ☐ Business income ☐ _____
- ☐ Blog income ☐ _____
- ☐ Foreign income ☐ _____
- ☐ Investment property income ☐ _____

EXPENSES

- ☐ Day Job ☐ _____
- ☐ Business ☐ _____
- ☐ Blog ☐ _____
- ☐ Investment property ☐ _____
- ☐ Charity ☐ _____
- ☐ Medical ☐ _____
- ☐ Interest paid on loans ☐ _____
- ☐ Child /Children relared expenses ☐ _____

Note: _____

_____

_____

− Tax Checklist −

Name _____

Financial Year _____

☐ Tax ID / social security number/ tax file number: _____
☐ Previous year's tax statements

INCOME

☐ Day Job   ☐ _____
☐ Bank account details   ☐ _____
☐ Bank statements   ☐ _____
☐ Dividends on investments   ☐ _____
☐ Business income   ☐ _____
☐ Blog income   ☐ _____
☐ Foreign income   ☐ _____
☐ Investment property income   ☐ _____

EXPENSES

☐ Day Job   ☐ _____
☐ Business   ☐ _____
☐ Blog   ☐ _____
☐ Investment property   ☐ _____
☐ Charity   ☐ _____
☐ Medical   ☐ _____
☐ Interest paid on loans   ☐ _____
☐ Child /Children relared expenses   ☐ _____

Note: _____

_____

_____

- Tax Checklist -

Name _____

Financial Year _____

- ☐ Tax ID / social security number/ tax file number: _____
- ☐ Previous year's tax statements

INCOME

- ☐ Day Job ☐ _____
- ☐ Bank account details ☐ _____
- ☐ Bank statements ☐ _____
- ☐ Dividends on investments ☐ _____
- ☐ Business income ☐ _____
- ☐ Blog income ☐ _____
- ☐ Foreign income ☐ _____
- ☐ Investment property income ☐ _____

EXPENSES

- ☐ Day Job ☐ _____
- ☐ Business ☐ _____
- ☐ Blog ☐ _____
- ☐ Investment property ☐ _____
- ☐ Charity ☐ _____
- ☐ Medical ☐ _____
- ☐ Interest paid on loans ☐ _____
- ☐ Child /Children relared expenses ☐ _____

Note: _____

_____

- Tax Checklist -

Name _____

Financial Year _____

- ☐ Tax ID / social security number/ tax file number: _____
- ☐ Previous year's tax statements

INCOME

- ☐ Day Job   ☐ _____
- ☐ Bank account details   ☐ _____
- ☐ Bank statements   ☐ _____
- ☐ Dividends on investments   ☐ _____
- ☐ Business income   ☐ _____
- ☐ Blog income   ☐ _____
- ☐ Foreign income   ☐ _____
- ☐ Investment property income   ☐ _____

EXPENSES

- ☐ Day Job   ☐ _____
- ☐ Business   ☐ _____
- ☐ Blog   ☐ _____
- ☐ Investment property   ☐ _____
- ☐ Charity   ☐ _____
- ☐ Medical   ☐ _____
- ☐ Interest paid on loans   ☐ _____
- ☐ Child /Children relared expenses   ☐ _____

Note: _____

_____

_____

– Tax Checklist –

Name _____

Financial Year _____

- ☐ Tax ID / social security number/ tax file number: _____
- ☐ Previous year's tax statements

INCOME

- ☐ Day Job   ☐ _____
- ☐ Bank account details   ☐ _____
- ☐ Bank statements   ☐ _____
- ☐ Dividends on investments   ☐ _____
- ☐ Business income   ☐ _____
- ☐ Blog income   ☐ _____
- ☐ Foreign income   ☐ _____
- ☐ Investment property income   ☐ _____

EXPENSES

- ☐ Day Job   ☐ _____
- ☐ Business   ☐ _____
- ☐ Blog   ☐ _____
- ☐ Investment property   ☐ _____
- ☐ Charity   ☐ _____
- ☐ Medical   ☐ _____
- ☐ Interest paid on loans   ☐ _____
- ☐ Child /Children relared expenses ☐ _____

Note: _____

_____

- Tax Checklist -

Name _____

Financial Year _____

- ☐ Tax ID / social security number/ tax file number: _____
- ☐ Previous year's tax statements

INCOME

- ☐ Day Job   ☐ _____
- ☐ Bank account details   ☐ _____
- ☐ Bank statements   ☐ _____
- ☐ Dividends on investments   ☐ _____
- ☐ Business income   ☐ _____
- ☐ Blog income   ☐ _____
- ☐ Foreign income   ☐ _____
- ☐ Investment property income   ☐ _____

EXPENSES

- ☐ Day Job   ☐ _____
- ☐ Business   ☐ _____
- ☐ Blog   ☐ _____
- ☐ Investment property   ☐ _____
- ☐ Charity   ☐ _____
- ☐ Medical   ☐ _____
- ☐ Interest paid on loans   ☐ _____
- ☐ Child /Children relared expenses ☐ _____

Note: _____

_____

_____

- *Tax Checklist* -

Name _____

Financial Year _____

- ☐ Tax ID / social security number/ tax file number: _____
- ☐ Previous year's tax statements

INCOME

- ☐ Day Job   ☐ _____
- ☐ Bank account details   ☐ _____
- ☐ Bank statements   ☐ _____
- ☐ Dividends on investments   ☐ _____
- ☐ Business income   ☐ _____
- ☐ Blog income   ☐ _____
- ☐ Foreign income   ☐ _____
- ☐ Investment property income   ☐ _____

EXPENSES

- ☐ Day Job   ☐ _____
- ☐ Business   ☐ _____
- ☐ Blog   ☐ _____
- ☐ Investment property   ☐ _____
- ☐ Charity   ☐ _____
- ☐ Medical   ☐ _____
- ☐ Interest paid on loans   ☐ _____
- ☐ Child /Children relared expenses   ☐ _____

Note: _____

- Tax Checklist -

Name _____

Financial Year _____

- ☐ Tax ID / social security number/ tax file number: _____
- ☐ Previous year's tax statements

INCOME

- ☐ Day Job ☐ _____
- ☐ Bank account details ☐ _____
- ☐ Bank statements ☐ _____
- ☐ Dividends on investments ☐ _____
- ☐ Business income ☐ _____
- ☐ Blog income ☐ _____
- ☐ Foreign income ☐ _____
- ☐ Investment property income ☐ _____

EXPENSES

- ☐ Day Job ☐ _____
- ☐ Business ☐ _____
- ☐ Blog ☐ _____
- ☐ Investment property ☐ _____
- ☐ Charity ☐ _____
- ☐ Medical ☐ _____
- ☐ Interest paid on loans ☐ _____
- ☐ Child /Children relared expenses ☐ _____

Note: _____

_____

_____

– Tax Checklist –

Name _____

Financial Year _____

- ☐ Tax ID / social security number/ tax file number: _____
- ☐ Previous year's tax statements

INCOME

- ☐ Day Job ☐ _____
- ☐ Bank account details ☐ _____
- ☐ Bank statements ☐ _____
- ☐ Dividends on investments ☐ _____
- ☐ Business income ☐ _____
- ☐ Blog income ☐ _____
- ☐ Foreign income ☐ _____
- ☐ Investment property income ☐ _____

EXPENSES

- ☐ Day Job ☐ _____
- ☐ Business ☐ _____
- ☐ Blog ☐ _____
- ☐ Investment property ☐ _____
- ☐ Charity ☐ _____
- ☐ Medical ☐ _____
- ☐ Interest paid on loans ☐ _____
- ☐ Child /Children relared expenses ☐ _____

Note: _____

- Tax Checklist -

Name _____

Financial Year _____

- ☐ Tax ID / social security number/ tax file number: _____
- ☐ Previous year's tax statements

INCOME

- ☐ Day Job   ☐ _____
- ☐ Bank account details   ☐ _____
- ☐ Bank statements   ☐ _____
- ☐ Dividends on investments   ☐ _____
- ☐ Business income   ☐ _____
- ☐ Blog income   ☐ _____
- ☐ Foreign income   ☐ _____
- ☐ Investment property income   ☐ _____

EXPENSES

- ☐ Day Job   ☐ _____
- ☐ Business   ☐ _____
- ☐ Blog   ☐ _____
- ☐ Investment property   ☐ _____
- ☐ Charity   ☐ _____
- ☐ Medical   ☐ _____
- ☐ Interest paid on loans   ☐ _____
- ☐ Child /Children relared expenses   ☐ _____

Note: _____

_____

- Tax Checklist -

Name _____

Financial Year _____

- ☐ Tax ID / social security number/ tax file number: _____
- ☐ Previous year's tax statements

INCOME

- ☐ Day Job ☐ _____
- ☐ Bank account details ☐ _____
- ☐ Bank statements ☐ _____
- ☐ Dividends on investments ☐ _____
- ☐ Business income ☐ _____
- ☐ Blog income ☐ _____
- ☐ Foreign income ☐ _____
- ☐ Investment property income ☐ _____

EXPENSES

- ☐ Day Job ☐ _____
- ☐ Business ☐ _____
- ☐ Blog ☐ _____
- ☐ Investment property ☐ _____
- ☐ Charity ☐ _____
- ☐ Medical ☐ _____
- ☐ Interest paid on loans ☐ _____
- ☐ Child /Children relared expenses ☐ _____

Note: _____

_____

- Tax Checklist -

Name _____

Financial Year _____

- ☐ Tax ID / social security number/ tax file number: _____
- ☐ Previous year's tax statements

INCOME

- ☐ Day Job — ☐ _____
- ☐ Bank account details — ☐ _____
- ☐ Bank statements — ☐ _____
- ☐ Dividends on investments — ☐ _____
- ☐ Business income — ☐ _____
- ☐ Blog income — ☐ _____
- ☐ Foreign income — ☐ _____
- ☐ Investment property income — ☐ _____

EXPENSES

- ☐ Day Job — ☐ _____
- ☐ Business — ☐ _____
- ☐ Blog — ☐ _____
- ☐ Investment property — ☐ _____
- ☐ Charity — ☐ _____
- ☐ Medical — ☐ _____
- ☐ Interest paid on loans — ☐ _____
- ☐ Child /Children relared expenses — ☐ _____

Note: _____
_____
_____

- Tax Checklist -

Name _____

Financial Year _____

- ☐ Tax ID / social security number/ tax file number: _____
- ☐ Previous year's tax statements

INCOME

- ☐ Day Job   ☐ _____
- ☐ Bank account details   ☐ _____
- ☐ Bank statements   ☐ _____
- ☐ Dividends on investments   ☐ _____
- ☐ Business income   ☐ _____
- ☐ Blog income   ☐ _____
- ☐ Foreign income   ☐ _____
- ☐ Investment property income   ☐ _____

EXPENSES

- ☐ Day Job   ☐ _____
- ☐ Business   ☐ _____
- ☐ Blog   ☐ _____
- ☐ Investment property   ☐ _____
- ☐ Charity   ☐ _____
- ☐ Medical   ☐ _____
- ☐ Interest paid on loans   ☐ _____
- ☐ Child /Children relared expenses   ☐ _____

Note: _____

_____

– Tax Checklist –

Name _____

Financial Year _____

- ☐ Tax ID / social security number/ tax file number: _____
- ☐ Previous year's tax statements

INCOME

- ☐ Day Job   ☐ _____
- ☐ Bank account details   ☐ _____
- ☐ Bank statements   ☐ _____
- ☐ Dividends on investments   ☐ _____
- ☐ Business income   ☐ _____
- ☐ Blog income   ☐ _____
- ☐ Foreign income   ☐ _____
- ☐ Investment property income   ☐ _____

EXPENSES

- ☐ Day Job   ☐ _____
- ☐ Business   ☐ _____
- ☐ Blog   ☐ _____
- ☐ Investment property   ☐ _____
- ☐ Charity   ☐ _____
- ☐ Medical   ☐ _____
- ☐ Interest paid on loans   ☐ _____
- ☐ Child /Children relared expenses   ☐ _____

Note: _____

_____

_____

— Tax Checklist —

Name _____

Financial Year _____

- ☐ Tax ID / social security number/ tax file number: _____
- ☐ Previous year's tax statements

INCOME

- ☐ Day Job   ☐ _____
- ☐ Bank account details   ☐ _____
- ☐ Bank statements   ☐ _____
- ☐ Dividends on investments   ☐ _____
- ☐ Business income   ☐ _____
- ☐ Blog income   ☐ _____
- ☐ Foreign income   ☐ _____
- ☐ Investment property income   ☐ _____

EXPENSES

- ☐ Day Job   ☐ _____
- ☐ Business   ☐ _____
- ☐ Blog   ☐ _____
- ☐ Investment property   ☐ _____
- ☐ Charity   ☐ _____
- ☐ Medical   ☐ _____
- ☐ Interest paid on loans   ☐ _____
- ☐ Child /Children relared expenses   ☐ _____

Note: _____

_____

_____

- Tax Checklist -

Name _____

Financial Year _____

- ☐ Tax ID / social security number/ tax file number: _____
- ☐ Previous year's tax statements

INCOME

- ☐ Day Job			☐ _____
- ☐ Bank account details	☐ _____
- ☐ Bank statements		☐ _____
- ☐ Dividends on investments	☐ _____
- ☐ Business income		☐ _____
- ☐ Blog income		☐ _____
- ☐ Foreign income		☐ _____
- ☐ Investment property income	☐ _____

EXPENSES

- ☐ Day Job			☐ _____
- ☐ Business			☐ _____
- ☐ Blog			☐ _____
- ☐ Investment property		☐ _____
- ☐ Charity			☐ _____
- ☐ Medical			☐ _____
- ☐ Interest paid on loans	☐ _____
- ☐ Child /Children relared expenses	☐ _____

Note: _____

_____

_____

- Tax Checklist -

Name _____

Financial Year _____

☐ Tax ID / social security number/ tax file number: _____

☐ Previous year's tax statements

INCOME

☐ Day Job ☐ _____
☐ Bank account details ☐ _____
☐ Bank statements ☐ _____
☐ Dividends on investments ☐ _____
☐ Business income ☐ _____
☐ Blog income ☐ _____
☐ Foreign income ☐ _____
☐ Investment property income ☐ _____

EXPENSES

☐ Day Job ☐ _____
☐ Business ☐ _____
☐ Blog ☐ _____
☐ Investment property ☐ _____
☐ Charity ☐ _____
☐ Medical ☐ _____
☐ Interest paid on loans ☐ _____
☐ Child /Children relared expenses ☐ _____

Note: _____

_____

- Tax Checklist -

Name _____

Financial Year _____

- ☐ Tax ID / social security number/ tax file number: _____
- ☐ Previous year's tax statements

INCOME

- ☐ Day Job   ☐ _____
- ☐ Bank account details   ☐ _____
- ☐ Bank statements   ☐ _____
- ☐ Dividends on investments   ☐ _____
- ☐ Business income   ☐ _____
- ☐ Blog income   ☐ _____
- ☐ Foreign income   ☐ _____
- ☐ Investment property income   ☐ _____

EXPENSES

- ☐ Day Job   ☐ _____
- ☐ Business   ☐ _____
- ☐ Blog   ☐ _____
- ☐ Investment property   ☐ _____
- ☐ Charity   ☐ _____
- ☐ Medical   ☐ _____
- ☐ Interest paid on loans   ☐ _____
- ☐ Child /Children relared expenses ☐ _____

Note: _____

_____

– Tax Checklist –

Name _____

Financial Year _____

- ☐ Tax ID / social security number/ tax file number: _____
- ☐ Previous year's tax statements

INCOME

- ☐ Day Job   ☐ _____
- ☐ Bank account details   ☐ _____
- ☐ Bank statements   ☐ _____
- ☐ Dividends on investments   ☐ _____
- ☐ Business income   ☐ _____
- ☐ Blog income   ☐ _____
- ☐ Foreign income   ☐ _____
- ☐ Investment property income   ☐ _____

EXPENSES

- ☐ Day Job   ☐ _____
- ☐ Business   ☐ _____
- ☐ Blog   ☐ _____
- ☐ Investment property   ☐ _____
- ☐ Charity   ☐ _____
- ☐ Medical   ☐ _____
- ☐ Interest paid on loans   ☐ _____
- ☐ Child /Children relared expenses ☐ _____

Note: _____

_____

- *Tax Checklist* -

Name _____

Financial Year _____

☐ Tax ID / social security number/ tax file number: _____

☐ Previous year's tax statements

INCOME

☐ Day Job   ☐ _____
☐ Bank account details   ☐ _____
☐ Bank statements   ☐ _____
☐ Dividends on investments   ☐ _____
☐ Business income   ☐ _____
☐ Blog income   ☐ _____
☐ Foreign income   ☐ _____
☐ Investment property income   ☐ _____

EXPENSES

☐ Day Job   ☐ _____
☐ Business   ☐ _____
☐ Blog   ☐ _____
☐ Investment property   ☐ _____
☐ Charity   ☐ _____
☐ Medical   ☐ _____
☐ Interest paid on loans   ☐ _____
☐ Child /Children relared expenses   ☐ _____

Note: _____

_____

− Tax Checklist −

Name _____

Financial Year _____

- ☐ Tax ID / social security number/ tax file number: _____
- ☐ Previous year's tax statements

INCOME

- ☐ Day Job ☐ _____
- ☐ Bank account details ☐ _____
- ☐ Bank statements ☐ _____
- ☐ Dividends on investments ☐ _____
- ☐ Business income ☐ _____
- ☐ Blog income ☐ _____
- ☐ Foreign income ☐ _____
- ☐ Investment property income ☐ _____

EXPENSES

- ☐ Day Job ☐ _____
- ☐ Business ☐ _____
- ☐ Blog ☐ _____
- ☐ Investment property ☐ _____
- ☐ Charity ☐ _____
- ☐ Medical ☐ _____
- ☐ Interest paid on loans ☐ _____
- ☐ Child /Children relared expenses ☐ _____

Note: _____

– Tax Checklist –

Name _____

Financial Year _____

- ☐ Tax ID / social security number/ tax file number: _____
- ☐ Previous year's tax statements

INCOME

- ☐ Day Job   ☐ _____
- ☐ Bank account details   ☐ _____
- ☐ Bank statements   ☐ _____
- ☐ Dividends on investments   ☐ _____
- ☐ Business income   ☐ _____
- ☐ Blog income   ☐ _____
- ☐ Foreign income   ☐ _____
- ☐ Investment property income   ☐ _____

EXPENSES

- ☐ Day Job   ☐ _____
- ☐ Business   ☐ _____
- ☐ Blog   ☐ _____
- ☐ Investment property   ☐ _____
- ☐ Charity   ☐ _____
- ☐ Medical   ☐ _____
- ☐ Interest paid on loans   ☐ _____
- ☐ Child /Children relared expenses   ☐ _____

Note: _____

_____

_____

- *Tax Checklist* -

Name _____

Financial Year _____

- ☐ Tax ID / social security number/ tax file number: _____
- ☐ Previous year's tax statements

INCOME

- ☐ Day Job ☐ _____
- ☐ Bank account details ☐ _____
- ☐ Bank statements ☐ _____
- ☐ Dividends on investments ☐ _____
- ☐ Business income ☐ _____
- ☐ Blog income ☐ _____
- ☐ Foreign income ☐ _____
- ☐ Investment property income ☐ _____

EXPENSES

- ☐ Day Job ☐ _____
- ☐ Business ☐ _____
- ☐ Blog ☐ _____
- ☐ Investment property ☐ _____
- ☐ Charity ☐ _____
- ☐ Medical ☐ _____
- ☐ Interest paid on loans ☐ _____
- ☐ Child /Children relared expenses ☐ _____

Note: _____

_____

- Tax Checklist -

Name _____

Financial Year _____

- ☐ Tax ID / social security number/ tax file number: _____
- ☐ Previous year's tax statements

INCOME

- ☐ Day Job   ☐ _____
- ☐ Bank account details ☐ _____
- ☐ Bank statements   ☐ _____
- ☐ Dividends on investments ☐ _____
- ☐ Business income   ☐ _____
- ☐ Blog income   ☐ _____
- ☐ Foreign income   ☐ _____
- ☐ Investment property income ☐ _____

EXPENSES

- ☐ Day Job   ☐ _____
- ☐ Business   ☐ _____
- ☐ Blog   ☐ _____
- ☐ Investment property ☐ _____
- ☐ Charity   ☐ _____
- ☐ Medical   ☐ _____
- ☐ Interest paid on loans ☐ _____
- ☐ Child /Children relared expenses ☐ _____

Note: _____

_____

- Tax Checklist -

Name _____

Financial Year _____

- ☐ Tax ID / social security number/ tax file number: _____
- ☐ Previous year's tax statements

INCOME

- ☐ Day Job ☐ _____
- ☐ Bank account details ☐ _____
- ☐ Bank statements ☐ _____
- ☐ Dividends on investments ☐ _____
- ☐ Business income ☐ _____
- ☐ Blog income ☐ _____
- ☐ Foreign income ☐ _____
- ☐ Investment property income ☐ _____

EXPENSES

- ☐ Day Job ☐ _____
- ☐ Business ☐ _____
- ☐ Blog ☐ _____
- ☐ Investment property ☐ _____
- ☐ Charity ☐ _____
- ☐ Medical ☐ _____
- ☐ Interest paid on loans ☐ _____
- ☐ Child /Children relared expenses ☐ _____

Note: _____

– Tax Checklist –

Name _____

Financial Year _____

- ☐ Tax ID / social security number/ tax file number: _____
- ☐ Previous year's tax statements

INCOME

- ☐ Day Job   ☐ _____
- ☐ Bank account details   ☐ _____
- ☐ Bank statements   ☐ _____
- ☐ Dividends on investments   ☐ _____
- ☐ Business income   ☐ _____
- ☐ Blog income   ☐ _____
- ☐ Foreign income   ☐ _____
- ☐ Investment property income   ☐ _____

EXPENSES

- ☐ Day Job   ☐ _____
- ☐ Business   ☐ _____
- ☐ Blog   ☐ _____
- ☐ Investment property   ☐ _____
- ☐ Charity   ☐ _____
- ☐ Medical   ☐ _____
- ☐ Interest paid on loans   ☐ _____
- ☐ Child /Children relared expenses ☐ _____

Note: _____

_____

_____

− Tax Checklist −

Name _____

Financial Year _____

- ☐ Tax ID / social security number/ tax file number: _____
- ☐ Previous year's tax statements

INCOME

- ☐ Day Job ☐ _____
- ☐ Bank account details ☐ _____
- ☐ Bank statements ☐ _____
- ☐ Dividends on investments ☐ _____
- ☐ Business income ☐ _____
- ☐ Blog income ☐ _____
- ☐ Foreign income ☐ _____
- ☐ Investment property income ☐ _____

EXPENSES

- ☐ Day Job ☐ _____
- ☐ Business ☐ _____
- ☐ Blog ☐ _____
- ☐ Investment property ☐ _____
- ☐ Charity ☐ _____
- ☐ Medical ☐ _____
- ☐ Interest paid on loans ☐ _____
- ☐ Child /Children relared expenses ☐ _____

Note: _____

_____

– Tax Checklist –

Name _____

Financial Year _____

- ☐ Tax ID / social security number/ tax file number: _____
- ☐ Previous year's tax statements

INCOME

- ☐ Day Job ☐ _____
- ☐ Bank account details ☐ _____
- ☐ Bank statements ☐ _____
- ☐ Dividends on investments ☐ _____
- ☐ Business income ☐ _____
- ☐ Blog income ☐ _____
- ☐ Foreign income ☐ _____
- ☐ Investment property income ☐ _____

EXPENSES

- ☐ Day Job ☐ _____
- ☐ Business ☐ _____
- ☐ Blog ☐ _____
- ☐ Investment property ☐ _____
- ☐ Charity ☐ _____
- ☐ Medical ☐ _____
- ☐ Interest paid on loans ☐ _____
- ☐ Child /Children relared expenses ☐ _____

Note: _____
_____
_____

- Tax Checklist -

Name _____

Financial Year _____

- ☐ Tax ID / social security number/ tax file number: _____
- ☐ Previous year's tax statements

INCOME

- ☐ Day Job   ☐ _____
- ☐ Bank account details   ☐ _____
- ☐ Bank statements   ☐ _____
- ☐ Dividends on investments   ☐ _____
- ☐ Business income   ☐ _____
- ☐ Blog income   ☐ _____
- ☐ Foreign income   ☐ _____
- ☐ Investment property income   ☐ _____

EXPENSES

- ☐ Day Job   ☐ _____
- ☐ Business   ☐ _____
- ☐ Blog   ☐ _____
- ☐ Investment property   ☐ _____
- ☐ Charity   ☐ _____
- ☐ Medical   ☐ _____
- ☐ Interest paid on loans   ☐ _____
- ☐ Child /Children relared expenses ☐ _____

Note: _____

– Tax Checklist –

Name _____

Financial Year _____

- ☐ Tax ID / social security number/ tax file number: _____
- ☐ Previous year's tax statements

INCOME

- ☐ Day Job   ☐ _____
- ☐ Bank account details   ☐ _____
- ☐ Bank statements   ☐ _____
- ☐ Dividends on investments   ☐ _____
- ☐ Business income   ☐ _____
- ☐ Blog income   ☐ _____
- ☐ Foreign income   ☐ _____
- ☐ Investment property income   ☐ _____

EXPENSES

- ☐ Day Job   ☐ _____
- ☐ Business   ☐ _____
- ☐ Blog   ☐ _____
- ☐ Investment property   ☐ _____
- ☐ Charity   ☐ _____
- ☐ Medical   ☐ _____
- ☐ Interest paid on loans   ☐ _____
- ☐ Child /Children relared expenses   ☐ _____

Note: _____
_____
_____

− Tax Checklist −

Name _____

Financial Year _____

- ☐ Tax ID / social security number/ tax file number: _____
- ☐ Previous year's tax statements

INCOME

- ☐ Day Job   ☐ _____
- ☐ Bank account details   ☐ _____
- ☐ Bank statements   ☐ _____
- ☐ Dividends on investments   ☐ _____
- ☐ Business income   ☐ _____
- ☐ Blog income   ☐ _____
- ☐ Foreign income   ☐ _____
- ☐ Investment property income   ☐ _____

EXPENSES

- ☐ Day Job   ☐ _____
- ☐ Business   ☐ _____
- ☐ Blog   ☐ _____
- ☐ Investment property   ☐ _____
- ☐ Charity   ☐ _____
- ☐ Medical   ☐ _____
- ☐ Interest paid on loans   ☐ _____
- ☐ Child /Children relared expenses ☐ _____

Note: _____

_____

- Tax Checklist -

Name _____

Financial Year _____

- ☐ Tax ID / social security number/ tax file number: _____
- ☐ Previous year's tax statements

INCOME

- ☐ Day Job   ☐ _____
- ☐ Bank account details   ☐ _____
- ☐ Bank statements   ☐ _____
- ☐ Dividends on investments   ☐ _____
- ☐ Business income   ☐ _____
- ☐ Blog income   ☐ _____
- ☐ Foreign income   ☐ _____
- ☐ Investment property income   ☐ _____

EXPENSES

- ☐ Day Job   ☐ _____
- ☐ Business   ☐ _____
- ☐ Blog   ☐ _____
- ☐ Investment property   ☐ _____
- ☐ Charity   ☐ _____
- ☐ Medical   ☐ _____
- ☐ Interest paid on loans   ☐ _____
- ☐ Child /Children relared expenses ☐ _____

Note:_____
_____

_____

- Tax Checklist -

Name _____

Financial Year _____

- ☐ Tax ID / social security number/ tax file number: _____
- ☐ Previous year's tax statements

INCOME

- ☐ Day Job
- ☐ Bank account details
- ☐ Bank statements
- ☐ Dividends on investments
- ☐ Business income
- ☐ Blog income
- ☐ Foreign income
- ☐ Investment property income

- ☐ _____
- ☐ _____
- ☐ _____
- ☐ _____
- ☐ _____
- ☐ _____
- ☐ _____
- ☐ _____

EXPENSES

- ☐ Day Job
- ☐ Business
- ☐ Blog
- ☐ Investment property
- ☐ Charity
- ☐ Medical
- ☐ Interest paid on loans
- ☐ Child /Children relared expenses

- ☐ _____
- ☐ _____
- ☐ _____
- ☐ _____
- ☐ _____
- ☐ _____
- ☐ _____
- ☐ _____

Note: _____
_____

- Tax Checklist -

Name _____

Financial Year _____

- ☐ Tax ID / social security number/ tax file number: _____
- ☐ Previous year's tax statements

INCOME

- ☐ Day Job   ☐ _____
- ☐ Bank account details   ☐ _____
- ☐ Bank statements   ☐ _____
- ☐ Dividends on investments   ☐ _____
- ☐ Business income   ☐ _____
- ☐ Blog income   ☐ _____
- ☐ Foreign income   ☐ _____
- ☐ Investment property income   ☐ _____

EXPENSES

- ☐ Day Job   ☐ _____
- ☐ Business   ☐ _____
- ☐ Blog   ☐ _____
- ☐ Investment property   ☐ _____
- ☐ Charity   ☐ _____
- ☐ Medical   ☐ _____
- ☐ Interest paid on loans   ☐ _____
- ☐ Child /Children relared expenses ☐ _____

Note: _____

_____

_____

- Tax Checklist -

Name _____

Financial Year _____

- ☐ Tax ID / social security number/ tax file number: _____
- ☐ Previous year's tax statements

INCOME

- ☐ Day Job   ☐ _____
- ☐ Bank account details   ☐ _____
- ☐ Bank statements   ☐ _____
- ☐ Dividends on investments   ☐ _____
- ☐ Business income   ☐ _____
- ☐ Blog income   ☐ _____
- ☐ Foreign income   ☐ _____
- ☐ Investment property income   ☐ _____

EXPENSES

- ☐ Day Job   ☐ _____
- ☐ Business   ☐ _____
- ☐ Blog   ☐ _____
- ☐ Investment property   ☐ _____
- ☐ Charity   ☐ _____
- ☐ Medical   ☐ _____
- ☐ Interest paid on loans   ☐ _____
- ☐ Child /Children relared expenses   ☐ _____

Note: _____

_____

- Tax Checklist -

Name _____

Financial Year _____

- ☐ Tax ID / social security number/ tax file number: _____
- ☐ Previous year's tax statements

INCOME

- ☐ Day Job ☐ _____
- ☐ Bank account details ☐ _____
- ☐ Bank statements ☐ _____
- ☐ Dividends on investments ☐ _____
- ☐ Business income ☐ _____
- ☐ Blog income ☐ _____
- ☐ Foreign income ☐ _____
- ☐ Investment property income ☐ _____

EXPENSES

- ☐ Day Job ☐ _____
- ☐ Business ☐ _____
- ☐ Blog ☐ _____
- ☐ Investment property ☐ _____
- ☐ Charity ☐ _____
- ☐ Medical ☐ _____
- ☐ Interest paid on loans ☐ _____
- ☐ Child /Children relared expenses ☐ _____

Note: _____
_____
_____

- *Tax Checklist* -

Name _____

Financial Year _____

- ☐ Tax ID / social security number/ tax file number: _____
- ☐ Previous year's tax statements

INCOME

- ☐ Day Job ☐ _____
- ☐ Bank account details ☐ _____
- ☐ Bank statements ☐ _____
- ☐ Dividends on investments ☐ _____
- ☐ Business income ☐ _____
- ☐ Blog income ☐ _____
- ☐ Foreign income ☐ _____
- ☐ Investment property income ☐ _____

EXPENSES

- ☐ Day Job ☐ _____
- ☐ Business ☐ _____
- ☐ Blog ☐ _____
- ☐ Investment property ☐ _____
- ☐ Charity ☐ _____
- ☐ Medical ☐ _____
- ☐ Interest paid on loans ☐ _____
- ☐ Child /Children relared expenses ☐ _____

Note: _____

_____

_____

- Tax Checklist -

Name _____

Financial Year _____

- ☐ Tax ID / social security number/ tax file number: _____
- ☐ Previous year's tax statements

INCOME

- ☐ Day Job   ☐ _____
- ☐ Bank account details   ☐ _____
- ☐ Bank statements   ☐ _____
- ☐ Dividends on investments   ☐ _____
- ☐ Business income   ☐ _____
- ☐ Blog income   ☐ _____
- ☐ Foreign income   ☐ _____
- ☐ Investment property income ☐ _____

EXPENSES

- ☐ Day Job   ☐ _____
- ☐ Business   ☐ _____
- ☐ Blog   ☐ _____
- ☐ Investment property   ☐ _____
- ☐ Charity   ☐ _____
- ☐ Medical   ☐ _____
- ☐ Interest paid on loans   ☐ _____
- ☐ Child /Children relared expenses ☐ _____

Note: _____

_____

_____

- *Tax Checklist* -

Name _____

Financial Year _____

☐ Tax ID / social security number/ tax file number: _____

☐ Previous year's tax statements

INCOME

☐ Day Job ☐ _____

☐ Bank account details ☐ _____

☐ Bank statements ☐ _____

☐ Dividends on investments ☐ _____

☐ Business income ☐ _____

☐ Blog income ☐ _____

☐ Foreign income ☐ _____

☐ Investment property income ☐ _____

EXPENSES

☐ Day Job ☐ _____

☐ Business ☐ _____

☐ Blog ☐ _____

☐ Investment property ☐ _____

☐ Charity ☐ _____

☐ Medical ☐ _____

☐ Interest paid on loans ☐ _____

☐ Child /Children relared expenses ☐ _____

Note: _____

_____

_____

- *Tax Checklist* -

Name _____

Financial Year _____

- ☐ Tax ID / social security number/ tax file number: _____
- ☐ Previous year's tax statements

INCOME

- ☐ Day Job   ☐ _____
- ☐ Bank account details   ☐ _____
- ☐ Bank statements   ☐ _____
- ☐ Dividends on investments   ☐ _____
- ☐ Business income   ☐ _____
- ☐ Blog income   ☐ _____
- ☐ Foreign income   ☐ _____
- ☐ Investment property income   ☐ _____

EXPENSES

- ☐ Day Job   ☐ _____
- ☐ Business   ☐ _____
- ☐ Blog   ☐ _____
- ☐ Investment property   ☐ _____
- ☐ Charity   ☐ _____
- ☐ Medical   ☐ _____
- ☐ Interest paid on loans   ☐ _____
- ☐ Child /Children relared expenses ☐ _____

Note: _____

_____

- Tax Checklist -

Name _____

Financial Year _____

- ☐ Tax ID / social security number/ tax file number: _____
- ☐ Previous year's tax statements

INCOME

- ☐ Day Job   ☐ _____
- ☐ Bank account details   ☐ _____
- ☐ Bank statements   ☐ _____
- ☐ Dividends on investments   ☐ _____
- ☐ Business income   ☐ _____
- ☐ Blog income   ☐ _____
- ☐ Foreign income   ☐ _____
- ☐ Investment property income   ☐ _____

EXPENSES

- ☐ Day Job   ☐ _____
- ☐ Business   ☐ _____
- ☐ Blog   ☐ _____
- ☐ Investment property   ☐ _____
- ☐ Charity   ☐ _____
- ☐ Medical   ☐ _____
- ☐ Interest paid on loans   ☐ _____
- ☐ Child /Children relared expenses ☐ _____

Note: _____

_____

– Tax Checklist –

Name _____

Financial Year _____

- ☐ Tax ID / social security number/ tax file number: _____
- ☐ Previous year's tax statements

INCOME

- ☐ Day Job
- ☐ Bank account details
- ☐ Bank statements
- ☐ Dividends on investments
- ☐ Business income
- ☐ Blog income
- ☐ Foreign income
- ☐ Investment property income

☐ _____
☐ _____
☐ _____
☐ _____
☐ _____
☐ _____
☐ _____
☐ _____

EXPENSES

- ☐ Day Job
- ☐ Business
- ☐ Blog
- ☐ Investment property
- ☐ Charity
- ☐ Medical
- ☐ Interest paid on loans
- ☐ Child /Children relared expenses

☐ _____
☐ _____
☐ _____
☐ _____
☐ _____
☐ _____
☐ _____
☐ _____

Note: _____
_____
_____

– Tax Checklist –

Name _____

Financial Year _____

- ☐ Tax ID / social security number/ tax file number: _____
- ☐ Previous year's tax statements

INCOME

- ☐ Day Job ☐ _____
- ☐ Bank account details ☐ _____
- ☐ Bank statements ☐ _____
- ☐ Dividends on investments ☐ _____
- ☐ Business income ☐ _____
- ☐ Blog income ☐ _____
- ☐ Foreign income ☐ _____
- ☐ Investment property income ☐ _____

EXPENSES

- ☐ Day Job ☐ _____
- ☐ Business ☐ _____
- ☐ Blog ☐ _____
- ☐ Investment property ☐ _____
- ☐ Charity ☐ _____
- ☐ Medical ☐ _____
- ☐ Interest paid on loans ☐ _____
- ☐ Child /Children relared expenses ☐ _____

Note: _____

- Tax Checklist -

Name _____

Financial Year _____

- ☐ Tax ID / social security number/ tax file number: _____
- ☐ Previous year's tax statements

INCOME

- ☐ Day Job ☐ _____
- ☐ Bank account details ☐ _____
- ☐ Bank statements ☐ _____
- ☐ Dividends on investments ☐ _____
- ☐ Business income ☐ _____
- ☐ Blog income ☐ _____
- ☐ Foreign income ☐ _____
- ☐ Investment property income ☐ _____

EXPENSES

- ☐ Day Job ☐ _____
- ☐ Business ☐ _____
- ☐ Blog ☐ _____
- ☐ Investment property ☐ _____
- ☐ Charity ☐ _____
- ☐ Medical ☐ _____
- ☐ Interest paid on loans ☐ _____
- ☐ Child /Children relared expenses ☐ _____

Note: _____
_____
_____

– Tax Checklist –

Name _____

Financial Year _____

- ☐ Tax ID / social security number/ tax file number: _____
- ☐ Previous year's tax statements

INCOME

- ☐ Day Job ☐ _____
- ☐ Bank account details ☐ _____
- ☐ Bank statements ☐ _____
- ☐ Dividends on investments ☐ _____
- ☐ Business income ☐ _____
- ☐ Blog income ☐ _____
- ☐ Foreign income ☐ _____
- ☐ Investment property income ☐ _____

EXPENSES

- ☐ Day Job ☐ _____
- ☐ Business ☐ _____
- ☐ Blog ☐ _____
- ☐ Investment property ☐ _____
- ☐ Charity ☐ _____
- ☐ Medical ☐ _____
- ☐ Interest paid on loans ☐ _____
- ☐ Child /Children relared expenses ☐ _____

Note: _____

- Tax Checklist -

Name _____

Financial Year _____

- ☐ Tax ID / social security number/ tax file number: _____
- ☐ Previous year's tax statements

INCOME

- ☐ Day Job
- ☐ Bank account details
- ☐ Bank statements
- ☐ Dividends on investments
- ☐ Business income
- ☐ Blog income
- ☐ Foreign income
- ☐ Investment property income

- ☐ _____
- ☐ _____
- ☐ _____
- ☐ _____
- ☐ _____
- ☐ _____
- ☐ _____
- ☐ _____

EXPENSES

- ☐ Day Job
- ☐ Business
- ☐ Blog
- ☐ Investment property
- ☐ Charity
- ☐ Medical
- ☐ Interest paid on loans
- ☐ Child /Children relared expenses

- ☐ _____
- ☐ _____
- ☐ _____
- ☐ _____
- ☐ _____
- ☐ _____
- ☐ _____
- ☐ _____

Note: _____

_____

_____

- Tax Checklist -

Name _____

Financial Year _____

- ☐ Tax ID / social security number/ tax file number: _____
- ☐ Previous year's tax statements

INCOME

- ☐ Day Job   ☐ _____
- ☐ Bank account details   ☐ _____
- ☐ Bank statements   ☐ _____
- ☐ Dividends on investments   ☐ _____
- ☐ Business income   ☐ _____
- ☐ Blog income   ☐ _____
- ☐ Foreign income   ☐ _____
- ☐ Investment property income   ☐ _____

EXPENSES

- ☐ Day Job   ☐ _____
- ☐ Business   ☐ _____
- ☐ Blog   ☐ _____
- ☐ Investment property   ☐ _____
- ☐ Charity   ☐ _____
- ☐ Medical   ☐ _____
- ☐ Interest paid on loans   ☐ _____
- ☐ Child /Children relared expenses   ☐ _____

Note: _____

_____

– Tax Checklist –

Name _____

Financial Year _____

- ☐ Tax ID / social security number/ tax file number: _____
- ☐ Previous year's tax statements

INCOME

- ☐ Day Job ☐ _____
- ☐ Bank account details ☐ _____
- ☐ Bank statements ☐ _____
- ☐ Dividends on investments ☐ _____
- ☐ Business income ☐ _____
- ☐ Blog income ☐ _____
- ☐ Foreign income ☐ _____
- ☐ Investment property income ☐ _____

EXPENSES

- ☐ Day Job ☐ _____
- ☐ Business ☐ _____
- ☐ Blog ☐ _____
- ☐ Investment property ☐ _____
- ☐ Charity ☐ _____
- ☐ Medical ☐ _____
- ☐ Interest paid on loans ☐ _____
- ☐ Child /Children relared expenses ☐ _____

Note: _____

_____

_____

- *Tax Checklist* -

Name _____

Financial Year _____

- ☐ Tax ID / social security number/ tax file number: _____
- ☐ Previous year's tax statements

INCOME

- ☐ Day Job ☐ _____
- ☐ Bank account details ☐ _____
- ☐ Bank statements ☐ _____
- ☐ Dividends on investments ☐ _____
- ☐ Business income ☐ _____
- ☐ Blog income ☐ _____
- ☐ Foreign income ☐ _____
- ☐ Investment property income ☐ _____

EXPENSES

- ☐ Day Job ☐ _____
- ☐ Business ☐ _____
- ☐ Blog ☐ _____
- ☐ Investment property ☐ _____
- ☐ Charity ☐ _____
- ☐ Medical ☐ _____
- ☐ Interest paid on loans ☐ _____
- ☐ Child /Children relared expenses ☐ _____

Note: _____

_____

_____

- Tax Checklist -

Name _____

Financial Year _____

- ☐ Tax ID / social security number/ tax file number: _____
- ☐ Previous year's tax statements

INCOME

- ☐ Day Job ☐ _____
- ☐ Bank account details ☐ _____
- ☐ Bank statements ☐ _____
- ☐ Dividends on investments ☐ _____
- ☐ Business income ☐ _____
- ☐ Blog income ☐ _____
- ☐ Foreign income ☐ _____
- ☐ Investment property income ☐ _____

EXPENSES

- ☐ Day Job ☐ _____
- ☐ Business ☐ _____
- ☐ Blog ☐ _____
- ☐ Investment property ☐ _____
- ☐ Charity ☐ _____
- ☐ Medical ☐ _____
- ☐ Interest paid on loans ☐ _____
- ☐ Child /Children relared expenses ☐ _____

Note: _____

_____

_____

- *Tax Checklist* -

Name _____

Financial Year _____

- ☐ Tax ID / social security number/ tax file number: _____
- ☐ Previous year's tax statements

INCOME

- ☐ Day Job   ☐ _____
- ☐ Bank account details   ☐ _____
- ☐ Bank statements   ☐ _____
- ☐ Dividends on investments   ☐ _____
- ☐ Business income   ☐ _____
- ☐ Blog income   ☐ _____
- ☐ Foreign income   ☐ _____
- ☐ Investment property income   ☐ _____

EXPENSES

- ☐ Day Job   ☐ _____
- ☐ Business   ☐ _____
- ☐ Blog   ☐ _____
- ☐ Investment property   ☐ _____
- ☐ Charity   ☐ _____
- ☐ Medical   ☐ _____
- ☐ Interest paid on loans   ☐ _____
- ☐ Child /Children relared expenses   ☐ _____

Note: _____

– Tax Checklist –

Name _____

Financial Year _____

- ☐ Tax ID / social security number/ tax file number: _____
- ☐ Previous year's tax statements

INCOME

- ☐ Day Job
- ☐ Bank account details
- ☐ Bank statements
- ☐ Dividends on investments
- ☐ Business income
- ☐ Blog income
- ☐ Foreign income
- ☐ Investment property income

☐ _____
☐ _____
☐ _____
☐ _____
☐ _____
☐ _____
☐ _____
☐ _____

EXPENSES

- ☐ Day Job
- ☐ Business
- ☐ Blog
- ☐ Investment property
- ☐ Charity
- ☐ Medical
- ☐ Interest paid on loans
- ☐ Child /Children relared expenses

☐ _____
☐ _____
☐ _____
☐ _____
☐ _____
☐ _____
☐ _____
☐ _____

Note: _____

_____

- Tax Checklist -

Name _____

Financial Year _____

- ☐ Tax ID / social security number/ tax file number: _____
- ☐ Previous year's tax statements

INCOME

- ☐ Day Job ☐ _____
- ☐ Bank account details ☐ _____
- ☐ Bank statements ☐ _____
- ☐ Dividends on investments ☐ _____
- ☐ Business income ☐ _____
- ☐ Blog income ☐ _____
- ☐ Foreign income ☐ _____
- ☐ Investment property income ☐ _____

EXPENSES

- ☐ Day Job ☐ _____
- ☐ Business ☐ _____
- ☐ Blog ☐ _____
- ☐ Investment property ☐ _____
- ☐ Charity ☐ _____
- ☐ Medical ☐ _____
- ☐ Interest paid on loans ☐ _____
- ☐ Child /Children relared expenses ☐ _____

Note: _____

- Tax Checklist -

Name _____

Financial Year _____

- ☐ Tax ID / social security number/ tax file number: _____
- ☐ Previous year's tax statements

INCOME

- ☐ Day Job ☐ _____
- ☐ Bank account details ☐ _____
- ☐ Bank statements ☐ _____
- ☐ Dividends on investments ☐ _____
- ☐ Business income ☐ _____
- ☐ Blog income ☐ _____
- ☐ Foreign income ☐ _____
- ☐ Investment property income ☐ _____

EXPENSES

- ☐ Day Job ☐ _____
- ☐ Business ☐ _____
- ☐ Blog ☐ _____
- ☐ Investment property ☐ _____
- ☐ Charity ☐ _____
- ☐ Medical ☐ _____
- ☐ Interest paid on loans ☐ _____
- ☐ Child /Children relared expenses ☐ _____

Note: _____

- *Tax Checklist* -

Name _____

Financial Year _____

- ☐ Tax ID / social security number/ tax file number: _____
- ☐ Previous year's tax statements

INCOME

- ☐ Day Job ☐ _____
- ☐ Bank account details ☐ _____
- ☐ Bank statements ☐ _____
- ☐ Dividends on investments ☐ _____
- ☐ Business income ☐ _____
- ☐ Blog income ☐ _____
- ☐ Foreign income ☐ _____
- ☐ Investment property income ☐ _____

EXPENSES

- ☐ Day Job ☐ _____
- ☐ Business ☐ _____
- ☐ Blog ☐ _____
- ☐ Investment property ☐ _____
- ☐ Charity ☐ _____
- ☐ Medical ☐ _____
- ☐ Interest paid on loans ☐ _____
- ☐ Child /Children relared expenses ☐ _____

Note: _____

- Tax Checklist -

Name _____

Financial Year _____

- ☐ Tax ID / social security number/ tax file number: _____
- ☐ Previous year's tax statements

INCOME

- ☐ Day Job ☐ _____
- ☐ Bank account details ☐ _____
- ☐ Bank statements ☐ _____
- ☐ Dividends on investments ☐ _____
- ☐ Business income ☐ _____
- ☐ Blog income ☐ _____
- ☐ Foreign income ☐ _____
- ☐ Investment property income ☐ _____

EXPENSES

- ☐ Day Job ☐ _____
- ☐ Business ☐ _____
- ☐ Blog ☐ _____
- ☐ Investment property ☐ _____
- ☐ Charity ☐ _____
- ☐ Medical ☐ _____
- ☐ Interest paid on loans ☐ _____
- ☐ Child /Children relared expenses ☐ _____

Note: _____

_____

– Tax Checklist –

Name _____

Financial Year _____

- ☐ Tax ID / social security number/ tax file number: _____
- ☐ Previous year's tax statements

INCOME

- ☐ Day Job   ☐ _____
- ☐ Bank account details   ☐ _____
- ☐ Bank statements   ☐ _____
- ☐ Dividends on investments   ☐ _____
- ☐ Business income   ☐ _____
- ☐ Blog income   ☐ _____
- ☐ Foreign income   ☐ _____
- ☐ Investment property income   ☐ _____

EXPENSES

- ☐ Day Job   ☐ _____
- ☐ Business   ☐ _____
- ☐ Blog   ☐ _____
- ☐ Investment property   ☐ _____
- ☐ Charity   ☐ _____
- ☐ Medical   ☐ _____
- ☐ Interest paid on loans   ☐ _____
- ☐ Child /Children relared expenses   ☐ _____

Note: _____

– Tax Checklist –

Name _____

Financial Year _____

- ☐ Tax ID / social security number/ tax file number: _____
- ☐ Previous year's tax statements

INCOME

- ☐ Day Job
- ☐ Bank account details
- ☐ Bank statements
- ☐ Dividends on investments
- ☐ Business income
- ☐ Blog income
- ☐ Foreign income
- ☐ Investment property income

☐ _____
☐ _____
☐ _____
☐ _____
☐ _____
☐ _____
☐ _____
☐ _____

EXPENSES

- ☐ Day Job
- ☐ Business
- ☐ Blog
- ☐ Investment property
- ☐ Charity
- ☐ Medical
- ☐ Interest paid on loans
- ☐ Child /Children relared expenses

☐ _____
☐ _____
☐ _____
☐ _____
☐ _____
☐ _____
☐ _____
☐ _____

Note: _____

_____

_____

- *Tax Checklist* -

Name _____

Financial Year _____

- ☐ Tax ID / social security number/ tax file number: _____
- ☐ Previous year's tax statements

INCOME

- ☐ Day Job
- ☐ Bank account details
- ☐ Bank statements
- ☐ Dividends on investments
- ☐ Business income
- ☐ Blog income
- ☐ Foreign income
- ☐ Investment property income

- ☐ _____
- ☐ _____
- ☐ _____
- ☐ _____
- ☐ _____
- ☐ _____
- ☐ _____
- ☐ _____

EXPENSES

- ☐ Day Job
- ☐ Business
- ☐ Blog
- ☐ Investment property
- ☐ Charity
- ☐ Medical
- ☐ Interest paid on loans
- ☐ Child /Children relared expenses

- ☐ _____
- ☐ _____
- ☐ _____
- ☐ _____
- ☐ _____
- ☐ _____
- ☐ _____
- ☐ _____

Note: _____
_____
_____

– Tax Checklist –

Name _____

Financial Year _____

- ☐ Tax ID / social security number/ tax file number: _____
- ☐ Previous year's tax statements

INCOME

- ☐ Day Job   ☐ _____
- ☐ Bank account details   ☐ _____
- ☐ Bank statements   ☐ _____
- ☐ Dividends on investments   ☐ _____
- ☐ Business income   ☐ _____
- ☐ Blog income   ☐ _____
- ☐ Foreign income   ☐ _____
- ☐ Investment property income   ☐ _____

EXPENSES

- ☐ Day Job   ☐ _____
- ☐ Business   ☐ _____
- ☐ Blog   ☐ _____
- ☐ Investment property   ☐ _____
- ☐ Charity   ☐ _____
- ☐ Medical   ☐ _____
- ☐ Interest paid on loans   ☐ _____
- ☐ Child /Children relared expenses ☐ _____

Note: _____

_____

- Tax Checklist -

Name _____

Financial Year _____

- ☐ Tax ID / social security number/ tax file number: _____
- ☐ Previous year's tax statements

INCOME

- ☐ Day Job
- ☐ Bank account details
- ☐ Bank statements
- ☐ Dividends on investments
- ☐ Business income
- ☐ Blog income
- ☐ Foreign income
- ☐ Investment property income

- ☐ _____
- ☐ _____
- ☐ _____
- ☐ _____
- ☐ _____
- ☐ _____
- ☐ _____
- ☐ _____

EXPENSES

- ☐ Day Job
- ☐ Business
- ☐ Blog
- ☐ Investment property
- ☐ Charity
- ☐ Medical
- ☐ Interest paid on loans
- ☐ Child /Children relared expenses

- ☐ _____
- ☐ _____
- ☐ _____
- ☐ _____
- ☐ _____
- ☐ _____
- ☐ _____
- ☐ _____

Note: _____

_____

_____

− Tax Checklist −

Name _____

Financial Year _____

- ☐ Tax ID / social security number/ tax file number: _____
- ☐ Previous year's tax statements

INCOME

- ☐ Day Job ☐ _____
- ☐ Bank account details ☐ _____
- ☐ Bank statements ☐ _____
- ☐ Dividends on investments ☐ _____
- ☐ Business income ☐ _____
- ☐ Blog income ☐ _____
- ☐ Foreign income ☐ _____
- ☐ Investment property income ☐ _____

EXPENSES

- ☐ Day Job ☐ _____
- ☐ Business ☐ _____
- ☐ Blog ☐ _____
- ☐ Investment property ☐ _____
- ☐ Charity ☐ _____
- ☐ Medical ☐ _____
- ☐ Interest paid on loans ☐ _____
- ☐ Child /Children relared expenses ☐ _____

Note: _____

_____

- Tax Checklist -

Name _____

Financial Year _____

- ☐ Tax ID / social security number/ tax file number: _____
- ☐ Previous year's tax statements

INCOME

- ☐ Day Job   ☐ _____
- ☐ Bank account details   ☐ _____
- ☐ Bank statements   ☐ _____
- ☐ Dividends on investments   ☐ _____
- ☐ Business income   ☐ _____
- ☐ Blog income   ☐ _____
- ☐ Foreign income   ☐ _____
- ☐ Investment property income   ☐ _____

EXPENSES

- ☐ Day Job   ☐ _____
- ☐ Business   ☐ _____
- ☐ Blog   ☐ _____
- ☐ Investment property   ☐ _____
- ☐ Charity   ☐ _____
- ☐ Medical   ☐ _____
- ☐ Interest paid on loans   ☐ _____
- ☐ Child /Children relared expenses ☐ _____

Note: _____

_____

_____

- Tax Checklist -

Name _____

Financial Year _____

- ☐ Tax ID / social security number/ tax file number: _____
- ☐ Previous year's tax statements

INCOME

- ☐ Day Job   ☐ _____
- ☐ Bank account details   ☐ _____
- ☐ Bank statements   ☐ _____
- ☐ Dividends on investments   ☐ _____
- ☐ Business income   ☐ _____
- ☐ Blog income   ☐ _____
- ☐ Foreign income   ☐ _____
- ☐ Investment property income   ☐ _____

EXPENSES

- ☐ Day Job   ☐ _____
- ☐ Business   ☐ _____
- ☐ Blog   ☐ _____
- ☐ Investment property   ☐ _____
- ☐ Charity   ☐ _____
- ☐ Medical   ☐ _____
- ☐ Interest paid on loans   ☐ _____
- ☐ Child /Children relared expenses   ☐ _____

Note: _____
_____
_____

- Tax Checklist -

Name _____

Financial Year _____

- ☐ Tax ID / social security number/ tax file number: _____
- ☐ Previous year's tax statements

INCOME

- ☐ Day Job   ☐ _____
- ☐ Bank account details   ☐ _____
- ☐ Bank statements   ☐ _____
- ☐ Dividends on investments ☐ _____
- ☐ Business income   ☐ _____
- ☐ Blog income   ☐ _____
- ☐ Foreign income   ☐ _____
- ☐ Investment property income ☐ _____

EXPENSES

- ☐ Day Job   ☐ _____
- ☐ Business   ☐ _____
- ☐ Blog   ☐ _____
- ☐ Investment property   ☐ _____
- ☐ Charity   ☐ _____
- ☐ Medical   ☐ _____
- ☐ Interest paid on loans   ☐ _____
- ☐ Child /Children relared expenses ☐ _____

Note: _____

− Tax Checklist −

Name _____

Financial Year _____

- ☐ Tax ID / social security number/ tax file number: _____
- ☐ Previous year's tax statements

INCOME

- ☐ Day Job ☐ _____
- ☐ Bank account details ☐ _____
- ☐ Bank statements ☐ _____
- ☐ Dividends on investments ☐ _____
- ☐ Business income ☐ _____
- ☐ Blog income ☐ _____
- ☐ Foreign income ☐ _____
- ☐ Investment property income ☐ _____

EXPENSES

- ☐ Day Job ☐ _____
- ☐ Business ☐ _____
- ☐ Blog ☐ _____
- ☐ Investment property ☐ _____
- ☐ Charity ☐ _____
- ☐ Medical ☐ _____
- ☐ Interest paid on loans ☐ _____
- ☐ Child /Children relared expenses ☐ _____

Note: _____

– Tax Checklist –

Name _____

Financial Year _____

- ☐ Tax ID / social security number/ tax file number: _____
- ☐ Previous year's tax statements

INCOME

- ☐ Day Job   ☐ _____
- ☐ Bank account details   ☐ _____
- ☐ Bank statements   ☐ _____
- ☐ Dividends on investments   ☐ _____
- ☐ Business income   ☐ _____
- ☐ Blog income   ☐ _____
- ☐ Foreign income   ☐ _____
- ☐ Investment property income   ☐ _____

EXPENSES

- ☐ Day Job   ☐ _____
- ☐ Business   ☐ _____
- ☐ Blog   ☐ _____
- ☐ Investment property   ☐ _____
- ☐ Charity   ☐ _____
- ☐ Medical   ☐ _____
- ☐ Interest paid on loans   ☐ _____
- ☐ Child /Children relared expenses ☐ _____

Note: _____

_____

_____

- Tax Checklist -

Name _____

Financial Year _____

- ☐ Tax ID / social security number/ tax file number: _____
- ☐ Previous year's tax statements

INCOME

- ☐ Day Job   ☐ _____
- ☐ Bank account details   ☐ _____
- ☐ Bank statements   ☐ _____
- ☐ Dividends on investments   ☐ _____
- ☐ Business income   ☐ _____
- ☐ Blog income   ☐ _____
- ☐ Foreign income   ☐ _____
- ☐ Investment property income   ☐ _____

EXPENSES

- ☐ Day Job   ☐ _____
- ☐ Business   ☐ _____
- ☐ Blog   ☐ _____
- ☐ Investment property   ☐ _____
- ☐ Charity   ☐ _____
- ☐ Medical   ☐ _____
- ☐ Interest paid on loans   ☐ _____
- ☐ Child /Children relared expenses ☐ _____

Note: _____

– Tax Checklist –

Name _____

Financial Year _____

- ☐ Tax ID / social security number/ tax file number: _____
- ☐ Previous year's tax statements

INCOME

- ☐ Day Job   ☐ _____
- ☐ Bank account details   ☐ _____
- ☐ Bank statements   ☐ _____
- ☐ Dividends on investments   ☐ _____
- ☐ Business income   ☐ _____
- ☐ Blog income   ☐ _____
- ☐ Foreign income   ☐ _____
- ☐ Investment property income   ☐ _____

EXPENSES

- ☐ Day Job   ☐ _____
- ☐ Business   ☐ _____
- ☐ Blog   ☐ _____
- ☐ Investment property   ☐ _____
- ☐ Charity   ☐ _____
- ☐ Medical   ☐ _____
- ☐ Interest paid on loans   ☐ _____
- ☐ Child /Children relared expenses   ☐ _____

Note: _____

_____

_____

www.ingramcontent.com/pod-product-compliance
Lightning Source LLC
Chambersburg PA
CBHW080549220526
45466CB00010B/3089